HOW GIRLS CAN HELP THEIR COUNTRY

THE FIRST ORIGINAL 1913
HANDBOOK FOR GIRL SCOUTS

BY **WALTER JOHN (W. J.) HOXIE**
FIRST PUBLISHED IN 1913

LEGACY EDITION

THE LIBRARY OF AMERICAN OUTDOORS

CLASSICS

BOOK 6

FEATURING

REMASTERED CLASSIC WORKS OF THE HIGHEST
QUALITY FROM **THE TIMELESS MASTERS AND
TEACHERS** OF CAMPING, OUTDOORS SKILLS,
WOODCRAFT, AND TRADITIONAL HANDCRAFTS

Doublebit Press
Eugene, OR

New content, introduction, and annotations
Copyright © 2019 by Doublebit Press. All rights reserved.

Doublebit Press is an imprint of Eagle Nest Press
www.doublebitpress.com | Eugene, OR, USA

Original text content under the public domain.
Originally published in 1913 by W.J. Hoxie & J. G. Low.

This title, along with other Doublebit Press books including the Library of American Outdoors Classics, are available at a volume discount for outdoors clubs or reading groups.

Doublebit Press Legacy Edition ISBNs
Hardcover: 978-1-64389-012-8
Paperback: 978-1-64389-013-5

Disclaimer: Because of its age and historic context, this text could contain content on present-day illegal outdoors activities, outdated medical information, or culturally and racially insensitive speech. Doublebit Press, or its employees, authors, and other affiliates, assume no liability for any actions performed by readers or any damages that might be related to information contained in this book. This text has been published for historical study and for personal literary enrichment toward the goal of the preservation of American outdoors history and heritage. Remember to be safe with any activity contained herein, respect your neighbors, and do your part to preserve and be a good steward of our great American wild lands.

First Doublebit Press Legacy Edition Printing, 2019

Printed in the United States of America
when purchased at retail in the USA

INTRODUCTION
To The Doublebit Press Legacy Edition

The founding of scout programs in America were inspired by Lord Robert Baden-Powell's scout movement in Britain, within which his sister Agnes Baden-Powell formed a program for girls called the Girl Guides. Seeing the successes of the Boy Scout program in America, Juliette Gordon Low founded the Girl Scouts. Like the Boy Scouts, much of early girl scouting was inspired by the British Girl Guides and the Baden-Powell family.

This book, *How Girls Can Help Their Country*, is the first original Handbook for Girl Scouts published in 1913. Author W. J. Hoxie is credited as having written it, although Juliette Gordon Low was instrumental in its publication as well. To this end, Hoxie worked closely with Low to organize the girl scout movement in the USA.

In this first version of the handbook, both Hoxie and Low borrowed heavily from Agnes Baden-Powell's girl guide handbook written at the time, and both Agnes and Lord Robert were credited on the title page. It seemed that at the time, borrowing heavily from books for youth was acceptable, as this occurred frequently with the Boy Scouts borrowing from books by Baden-Powell, Ernest Thompson Seton, and Daniel Carter Beard, just to name a few.

This book includes the first girl scout requirements for badges and proficiency tests, as well as instruction on a number of topics. These include outdoors craft and camping, first aid, water skills, home living, patriotism and citizenship, and cooking. Go back in time when girl scouts made food, fires, and their outdoors equipment from scratch, and had to navigate the wilderness to find their campsites. This book is full of timeless knowledge, much of which has not been found in texts for decades!

Remember, though, to stay safe, and don't do anything dangerous! Although it contains interesting information and describes multiple traditional skills and activities, many activities and ideas that were presented in this 1913 edition are now considered either unsafe or unacceptable (such as ditching a tent or chopping down live trees). Please respect your campsite, your neighbors, and yourself as you try some of the activities of original scouts - be prepared and be safe!

Look back on this fascinating era with a historic eye and imagine what it was like to be a scout when the program was just starting! As a whole, this book gives a fascinating look at scouting of the birth of the movement. The types of tests and skills that both girl and boy scouts were required to perform to receive badges were quite involved, and perhaps much more difficult for modern scouts to perform today. This book represents classic scouting at its finest! Try your best to perform some of the skills in this book - you may find that many of the activities described within are harder than they seem!

About the Library of American Outdoors Classics

The old experts of the woods and mountains taught timeless principles and skills for decades. Through their books, the old experts offered rich descriptions of the outdoor world and encouraged learning through personal experiences in nature. Over the last 125 years, camping, outdoors recreation, and woods activities have substantially changed. Many things have gotten simpler as gear has improved, and life outside or on the trail now brings with it many of the same comforts enjoyed in town. In addition, some activities of the olden days are now no longer in vogue, or are even outright considered inappropriate or illegal, such as high-impact camping practices like chopping down live trees. However, despite many of the positive changes in outdoors methods that have occurred over the years, *there are many other skills and much knowledge that have been forgotten* from the golden era of American outdoors recreation.

By publishing the Library of American Outdoors Classics, it is our goal at Doublebit Press to do what we can to preserve and share the works from forgotten teachers that form the cornerstone of the history of the American outdoors. Through remastered reprint editions of timeless classics of outdoor recreation, perhaps we can regain some of this lost knowledge for future generations.

Because there were fewer options for finding outdoors gear in the early 1900's, experts in *"woodcraft"* skills (not to be confused with today's use of the word to mean woodworking or making things of wood) had to have a deep knowledge of the basic building blocks of outdoor living. This involved not only surviving in the outdoors, but to also have a comfortable and enjoyable time. As Nessmuk puts it in his book *Woodcraft,* "We do not go to the woods to rough it; we go to smooth it — we get it rough enough in town. But let us live the simple, natural life in the woods, and leave all frills behind." Nessmuk did not advocate for folks to go outside and have a terrible time. That would be contrary to the whole point of getting outside. Instead, he advocated for a "simpler" life by leaving some of the creature comforts of the city behind, but also entering the outdoors in a smart and practiced way that made the experience a much more satisfying vacation from home. The goal is to be comfortable so you can focus on having a good time outside and take in everything exposure to nature can offer. However, to be comfortable, one has to know the ins and outs of camping and outdoors life. Despite all the advances in campcraft and outdoors recreation, the old masters of the woods would all likely argue that this will only come from practicing the basics.

Because there was no market yet for specialty outdoors recreational gear (and thus, few outfitters), most outdoors gear came from military surplus piles or was custom made. As such, the old masters of woodcraft often made their own gear suited to their tastes. Through much experience in the woods and field, the great outdoors experts had to know why things worked the way they did by understanding the great web of cause and effect in nature. They had to learn from experience why certain gear worked better in different conditions or know how to solve problems off-the-cuff when things got hairy. They used the basic blocks of camping and outdoors knowledge to fine-tune their gear. They gained experience whenever they could and tried things different ways so they could gain mastery over the fundamentals and see challenges from many angles.

Today, much of the outdoor experience has been greatly simplified by neatly arranged campsites at public campgrounds and gear that has been meticulously improved and tested in both the lab and the field. Many modern conveniences are only a brief trek away, with many parks, campgrounds, and even forests having easy-access roads, convenience stores, and even cell phone signal. In some ways, it is much easier to camp and go outdoors today, and that is a good thing! We should not be miserable when we go outside — lovers of the outdoors know the essential restorative capability that the woods can have on the body, mind, and soul. Although things have gotten easier on us in the 21st Century when it comes to the outdoors, it certainly does not mean that we should forget the foundations of outdoors lore, though. All modern camping skills, outdoors equipment, and cool gizmos that make our lives easier are all founded on principles of the outdoors that the old masters knew well and taught to those who would listen.

Every woods master had their own curriculum or thought some things were more important than others. This includes the present author — certain things appear in this book that other masters leave out of theirs. The old masters also taught common things in slightly different ways or did things differently than others. That's what makes each of the experts different and worth reading. There's no universal way of doing something, especially now. Learning to go about something differently helps with mastery or learn a new skill altogether. Again, to use the metaphor from the above paragraphs, outdoors skills mastery consists of learning the basic building blocks of outdoors living, woods and nature lore, and the art of packing properly for trips. Each master goes about describing these building blocks differently or shows a different aspect of them.

Therefore, we have decided to publish this Legacy Edition in our Library of American Outdoors Classics series. This book is an important contribution to the early American recreational outdoors literature and has important historical and collector value toward preserving the American outdoors tradition. The knowledge it holds is an invaluable reference for practicing skills and hand craft methods. Its chapters thoroughly discuss some of the essential building blocks of knowledge that are fundamental but may have been forgotten as equipment gets fancier and technology gets smarter. In short, this book was chosen for Legacy Edition printing because much of the basic skills and knowledge it contains has been forgotten or put to the wayside in trade for more modern conveniences and methods.

Although the editors at Doublebit Press are thrilled to have comfortable experiences in the woods and love our high-tech and light-weight equipment, we are also realizing that the basic skills taught by the old masters are more essential than ever as our culture becomes more and more hooked on digital stuff. We don't want to risk forgetting the important steps, skills, or building blocks involved with thriving in the outdoors. The Legacy Edition series represents the essential contributions to the American outdoors tradition by the great experts of outdoors life and traditional hand crafting.

With technology playing a major role in everyday life, sometimes we need to take a step back in time to find those basic building blocks used for gaining mastery – the things that we have luckily not completely lost and has been recorded in books over the last two centuries. These skills aren't forgotten, they've just been shelved. *It's time to unshelve them once again and reclaim the lost knowledge of self-sufficiency.*

Based on this commitment to preserving our outdoors and handcraft heritage, we have taken great pride in publishing this book as a complete original work. We hope it is worthy of both study and collection by outdoors folk in the modern era of outdoors and traditional skills life.

Unlike many other photocopy reproductions of classic books that are common on the market, this Legacy Edition does not simply place poor photography of old texts on our pages and use error-prone optical scanning or computer-generated text. We want our work to speak for itself, and reflect the quality demanded by our customers who spend their hard-earned money. With this in mind, each Legacy Edition book that has been chosen for publication is carefully remastered from original print books, *with the Doublebit Legacy Edition printed and laid out in the exact way that it was presented at its original publication.* We provide a beautiful, memorable experience that is as true to the original text as best as possible, but with the aid of modern technology to make as beautiful a reading experience as possible for books that are typically over a century old.

Because of its age and because it is presented in its original form, the book may contain misspellings, inking errors, and other print blemishes that were common for the age. However, these are exactly the things that we feel give the book its character, which we preserved in this Legacy Edition. During digitization, we ensured that each illustration in the text was clean and sharp with the least amount of loss from being copied and digitized as possible. Full-page plate illustrations are presented as they were found, often including the extra blank page that was often behind a plate. For the covers, we use the original cover design to give the book its original feel. We are sure you'll appreciate the fine touches and attention to detail that your Legacy Edition has to offer.

For outdoors enthusiasts who demand the best from their equipment, this Doublebit Press Legacy Edition reprint was made with you in mind. Both important and minor details have equally both been accounted for by our publishing staff, down to the cover, font, layout, and images. It is the goal of Doublebit Legacy Edition series to preserve outdoors heritage, but also be cherished as collectible pieces, worthy of collection in any outdoorsperson's library and that can be passed to future generations.

Every book selected to be in this series offers unique views and instruction on important skills, advice, tips, tidbits, anecdotes, stories, and experiences that will enrich the repertoire of any person who enjoys escaping the city and finding their way to the trails of the wilds. To learn the most basic building blocks of outdoors life leads to mastery of all its aspects.

Placing Outdoors Classics in Their Historical Times

Enjoying the outdoors is an American tradition! As such, our goal with the Legacy Edition printings of our Library of American Outdoors Classics Series is to preserve this tradition for future generations by preserving the knowledge of the old masters of the craft. Part of enjoying the outdoors today is the need to practice careful stewardship for our wild lands, as well as focus on our own safety. For years, outdoors groups such as the Scouts or sportsmen's associations have taught folks how to enjoy the outdoors and practice traditional skills in a safe and responsible manner. We extend this same challenge to those who read our remastered books.

Authors used to write with a stupendous number of extra words and grand, superfluous prose back in the day! How dreadfully verbose! Some of the words and phrases used by the author, or the views expressed by the author, can also be outdated by today's standards.

Because this book was written in a different age, ideas in this text could also be insensitive to some people given today's language use and societal norms. This is not to say that everything in old camping books is politically incorrect (which, of course, it likely is), but instead that it just may sound weird to modern readers.

As such, you should read this book with an idea for the time in which it was written. Language and perspectives change over the centuries. To understand the written knowledge of previous eras, we have to take the language they used in stride and think about what it was like in the early 1900's. We can read historic books within the contexts and times in which they were written. Despite authors perhaps having some outdated social views, these old texts still have plenty to teach and can impart knowledge that has been long lost by today's standards!

In addition to odd language or obsolete ideas, *this book may describe some activities that are incompatible with today's standards of outdoor ethics, consideration for other outdoorspeople, conservation, ecology, and the Leave No Trace philosophy of outdoors recreation.* We can't stress enough: because this book was published decades ago, there are some things in it that are irresponsible, inappropriate, dangerous, or outright illegal today. Forests and forest management have changed a lot since 1900. There is far more caution placed today on the preservation of forests and prevention of fire than in the early 20th Century. Because of this, we caution readers to pay close attention regarding safety, conservation, or legality, particularly include the use of fire, cutting live trees or plants, digging holes, use of firearms or potentially dangerous tools, killing of animals, or activities involving survival in the wilderness, especially when alone. Some activities in this book may even be illegal in some areas, especially public areas such as parks, National Forests, and designated wilderness areas. Even on private property, old outdoors activities and skills can remain dangerous. Any hunting, fishing, or trapping should always be done with proper licenses and training, and within the bounds of the law. When trying new activities from this book, it should be done under the supervision of experts and with a focus on the safety of everyone involved.

We also encourage youth to grab this book and learn from it! Start while you're young! If you're a curious kid or teen who finds the outdoors fascinating and want to become an outdoors expert, the activities in this book should give you a great education in the old woods skills. However, these activities should also be done alongside parents' or qualified adult supervision. We're not trying to be boring or kill the fun - quite the opposite. We believe that youth should have chances to get outside and learn the fun stuff the old woods experts offer to teach in their books. It's just best to consult with adults when doing some of the activities in this book, especially if they are new to you.

It is also useful to check with outdoors stewardship organizations and governments about what outdoors practices are allowed and which are either not or otherwise discouraged. Examples of organizations dedicated to outdoors stewardship include the Leave No Trace Center for Outdoors Ethics, The Mountaineers, The Boy Scouts of America, The Girl Scouts of America, American Hiking Society, Appalachian Mountain Club, Tread Lightly!, and The Sierra Club. Many of these groups' websites have plenty of information about proper outdoors practices and ethics for preserving our great outdoors heritage and lands.

Specifically, a visit to your local US Forest Service, Bureau of Land Management, or State Fish and Wildlife Management offices should also point you in the right direction toward questions about regulations, permits, and proper outdoors behavior on public lands.

Finally, Doublebit Press is committed to expanding the access to information for everyone about outdoors mastery, DIY and self-sufficient skills, "simpler" living (said in quotes because the so-called *simple life* can be quite complex), and reflections on the lives of the old master outdoorsfolk. Despite this goal, it is unfortunate that the original texts that we publish most frequently only mention men or boys. It's as if women or girls never wanted to go outside for over a century (hint: it's just not true.) The history of the last two centuries is full of examples of women and girls who found the outdoors restorative, educative, and empowering, such as with the great programs of the Camp Fire Girls and the Girl Scouts. It's an unfortunate aspect of American outdoors history that the outside world was not inviting to everyone. Those who desire to reflect on life's complexities through the simplicity of the outdoors should make this knowledge their own, even if authors were too shortsighted to include everyone in their original texts, or even outright talk down to women who wanted to be outside. We're not trying to be politically correct here, but instead to encourage everyone to get outside and enjoy its benefits.

Studying This Book

The pages within this book present an overwhelming amount of information, facts, and directions to memorize that are often outdated and at the least, out of practice by modern standards. That doesn't mean that these pages have nothing to teach! It's just going to likely be new stuff for many readers.

Our one suggestion is *don't try to memorize everything,* especially when you're thumbing through the book or even reading it cover-to-cover. Writings from the late 1800's to early 1900's can be dense and out of style for someone not used to reading these types of books. Instead, gain some basic familiarity with each topic by thumbing through the pages, looking at the illustrations, and seeing the section headers. Then, choose a few topics or skills at a single time for deeper study.

Before camping or other outdoors trips can even begin, some planning and reflection is useful, which may be best done in town before you go out to the field. First, it might be helpful to read through the book with plans in mind. The book can provide useful material for close study and reflection when in town before you head out to the field to practice.

Secondly, once you've come up with a practice plan, you will of course want to start doing tasks and skills in the field. Doublebit Legacy books and the Library of American Outdoors Classics represents many field skills to master that have long sense been out of practice, but hopefully not forgotten! These include making and trying different kinds of tents or shelters, cooking (including any fish and game caught by you in the field), making many types of fires, setting up camp to suit your personal needs, beating the bugs and elements, understanding the terrain and weather, making furniture, brushing up on your nature lore, emergency survival, and testing your personal outfit and tools.

Any of the old tutors of woodcraft will tell you in their classic books that you can only truly learn how to go camping and do woodcraft by *actually doing it*. Home study indeed does you well by using the many guidebooks that have been published over the previous 125 years. However, hundreds more lessons will become immediately available to you the moment you start with some of the old-style tasks. This old style of outdoorsing is indeed outdated in many ways, but the approach still has much to teach modern campers who have become accustomed to carved out campsites, cabin and RV camping, and high-tech equipment.

Before the days of outfitters, outdoors adventurers made their gear, which was tailored to their individual needs. Many experiments were done in the field to tweak their gear to get that ever-changing point of "perfect." Aside from experiencing wonderful lessons in history, getting outside and doing some of the activities this book will give you an appreciation for modern advances in outdoors and handcraft method and tools of the trade, as well as a deeper understanding of the foundations of outdoors and handcraft life in the event that your gear fails you or you otherwise find yourself in situations where knowing the principles will get you unstuck fast.

If we were to tally up each of the individual tips in the Doublebit Library of American Outdoors Classics, they would easily number in the thousands. The old masters represent centuries of previous knowledge that have been all but lost to 21st Century, technology-driven folks. To this point, although experience and *actually doing stuff* are the best forms of learning, taking a mindful approach to study of these works also benefit your development as a competent outdoorsperson and handcrafter. You can study alone but working with a friend or travel companion can also help you both learn even more from your companions' experiences!

You may also find it invaluable to take these volumes with you on your camping or other outdoors trips. In addition to having reading material on a variety of topics in the field for down time, you'll also find a thousand things to try in these pages if you're bored. Although skills may be best studied when in the field through experience and reflection, you may also study woods skills at home as well. Gaining familiarity through reading, videos, and other media are a great start toward building your ability toward gaining mastery in the field.

So, without blabbering on further, we hope you enjoy your Doublebit Legacy Edition. May your trails be clear and your experiences be memorable!

- The Doublebit Press Editors

A GIRL SCOUT.

How Girls Can Help Their Country

By

W. J. Hoxie

Adapted from the Handbook

By

Agnes Baden-Powell

and

Sir Robert Baden-Powell

The Knickerbocker Press
New York
1913

COPYRIGHT, 1913
BY
JULIETTE LOW

Contents

PAGE

Part I. Summary.

How to Start a Patrol	1
First Meeting	2
Girl-Scout Law	3
Second Meeting	7
Duties	12

Part II. Camping. 18

Open-Air Pursuits	33
Self-Defence	41
Woodcraft	44
Botany	51
Stars	51
Gardening	63

Part III. Home Life.

Sanitation	66
Housewifery	77
Cooking	80
Care of Children	86

CONTENTS

	PAGE
Part IV. Hospital Work.	90
Tending the Injured	91
Be Prepared for Accidents	91
Part V. Patriotism.	102
Self-Discipline	106
Self-Improvement	108
Part VI. Organization.	119
Qualifications for Three Ranks of Scouts	123
Ceremony of Investiture	125
Tests for Proficiency Badges	129
Notes to Instructors	142

FOREWORD

If character training and learning citizenship are necessary for boys, how much more important it is that these principles should be instilled into the minds of girls who are destined to be the mothers and guides of the next generation. An attractive and practical form of active educational pastime is needed and for this purpose the Girl Scouts are organized. The Scout movement, so popular among boys, is unfitted for the needs of girls, but on something the same lines has been devised the present system giving a more womanly training for both mind and body.

Honor, duty, loyalty, kindness, comradeship, purity, cheerfulness, and thrift, are the qualities it seeks to develop.

To be a Girl Scout, a girl should love and admire these things in other people, seek to attain them herself, and to promote them among her comrades, not in any priggish fashion, but through being loyal, honorable, kind, and helpful, in the home, in the school, in the field, on the playground, and in the Club Room.

Abstract talks about these qualities mean little to youth.

Because this is so, a set of definite laws is given to the leaders to be read at their own discretion to the girls as practical definition of what it means to be honorable, loyal, helpful, etc.

When a leader has come to know a girl, and the girl has become well known to the other girls, if, in the opinion of the leader, she has become fine and strong enough to meet the requirements of the law, she may be permitted, if she so desires, to promise to do her best to keep the law and so become a Girl Scout eligible to qualify for any Scout rank.

The Captain should remember that simple living in the spirit of this law is more important than being able to state the law and talk glibly about it. Children learn more from imitation and from the right ordering of their experiences than they do from any amount of didactic teaching.

A Captain should avoid preaching and formalism. She should live with her girls in a happy, helpful, wholesome, honorable spirit and so promote the same spirit in the patrol. The finer girls in the patrol will do the rest, and youth will be led by the formative and compelling power of example.

Some reference to the Boy Scouts book may be of service to the instructors but should not be followed too closely. Good womanly common-sense will be a sure guide as to how far to go with it. And in America we have in some parts of our big country problems to meet that are unknown abroad. In some parts of the country too much actual scouting cannot be indulged in except under competent protection.

Among girls there are wide class distinctions—much wider than among boys. The character training of the Scouts seems to bring these classes if not actually closer together at least much more in sympathy. It is unnecessary and perhaps injurious to obliterate them altogether. All being Scouts brings about a kindly sympathy and unity of aims.

How Girls Can Help Their Country

How Girls Can Help Their Country
Part I

SUMMARY

It is not intended that Girl Scouts should form a new club, separated from all others, but that girls who belong to any kind of existing organization, such as school clubs, factories, social or charitable clubs, Y. W. C. A's., can also take up, in addition to their other work or play, the Girl Scouts' training and games, especially on Saturdays and Sundays.

By meeting on Sundays it is not meant that girls should play or work, but that they should take walks where they can carry out Nature study of plants and animals, that is, of God's work in nature, and to do good turns.

Where girls do not already belong to any clubs, they can form themselves into groups and bands, and these are called Girl Scouts.

How to Start a Patrol

Eight girls in any town, school, or settlement join together to form a Patrol. They should have a Captain who must be at least twenty-one years old. She selects a Lieutenant, or second in command, and the girls elect one of themselves as Patrol leader. The girls are usually from ten to seventeen years of age. It is best if all the girls in each Patrol are about the same age.

Notes to Instructors

(Any paragraph printed in italics in this book is addressed to Instructors.)

If your Scouts are to enjoy their training you must enjoy it too. Keep on a smile but never let it be a smile of contempt. Have sympathy with failure not censure. "Hate nothing but sin."

Illustrate and explain before attempting to drill and do not drill too long. Practice makes perfect but not exhaustion. Games should be selected carefully. Reject all that carry a sting with them, as too many games are apt to do. Being "it" should be a reward and a privilege—never a punishment or rebuke for poor work or failure.

So of competitions. Take away the sting of failure as much as possible from the defeated ones.

Practices, games, and competitions being so large a part of Scouts' training, it is of course necessary to have rules that must be always obeyed on any and all occasions. This is one of the most important principles to be instilled: strict and prompt obedience to laws and orders. Consent of parents or guardian should come before enrollment of a Scout. Each girl will be a study by herself, and her talents may be improved in the best possible direction. A Captain is first and foremost a teacher. Before disbanding, a Captain should select two girls as Orderlies for different duties, such as tidying the club room and leaving everything in order.

Dismiss in good time. Captains are responsible for the members of their patrols going home. They should not be kept too late.

THE FIRST MEETING

At their first meeting the Scouts are all enrolled and form patrols; each one should have a note-book, pencil, and a yard of cord, and they are taught the Scouts' Promise.

THE LAWS OF THE SCOUTS. Scouts the world over have unwritten laws which are just as binding upon them as if they were printed in black and white. Their origin is lost in the mists of ancient history.

The Japanese have their laws of the old Samurai warriors; we have the laws of the Chivalry of the days "when Knighthood was in power." Our American Indian has his Calumet and the Arab respects the guest who has eaten his salt. All have their ancient codes of moral laws.

The following are the rules which apply to Girl Scouts. After six months probation a girl can promise to try to live up to this promise.

Girl Scout's Promise

Each girl must promise on her honor to try to do three things:

1. **To do your duty to God and to your country.**
2. **To help other people at all times.**
3. **To obey the Laws of the Scouts.**

They learn the salute and the secret sign of the Scouts. (For a full description of the investment of the Scouts, the tests for the three grades of Girl Scouts, Tenderfoot, Second Class, and First Class Girl Scouts, see pages 123–125.)

The Salute

These laws are for the guidance of Captains and the girls are not given the Law until the Captain considers they are capable of living up to the spirit of the Law.

THE GIRL SCOUT LAW

1. A Girl Scout's Honor Is to be Trusted

If a Scout says, "on my honor it is so," that means that what she says is as true as if she had taken a most solemn oath. In fact a Scout need never take any other form of oath.

2. A Girl Scout Is Loyal

to the President, to her country, and to her officers; to her father, to her mother, and to her employers. She must stick to them through thick and thin against any one who is their enemy, or even who talks badly of them.

3. A Girl Scout's Duty Is to be Useful and to Help Others

She is to do her duty before anything else even if she gives up her own pleasure, safety, or comfort to do it. When in doubt as to which of two things to do she must think, "Which is my duty?" which means, "Which is the best for other people?"—and do that at once. She must be prepared at any time to save life or help the injured. She should do at least one good turn to somebody every day.

4. A Girl Scout Is a Friend to All, and a Sister to every Other Girl Scout no Matter to what Social Class she May Belong

Thus if a Scout meet another Scout, even though a stranger to her, she may speak to her, and help her in any way she can, either to carry out the duty she is then doing or by giving her food, or as far as possible anything she may want. Like Kim a Scout should be "Little friend to all the world."

5. A Girl Scout Is Courteous

That is, she is polite to all but especially to old people and invalids, cripples, etc. She must not take any reward for being helpful or courteous.

6. A Girl Scout Keeps herself Pure

in thought and word and deed.

7. A Girl Scout Is a Friend to Animals

She should save them as far as possible from pain and should not kill even the smallest unnecessarily. They are all God's creatures.

8. A Girl Scout Obeys Orders

Under all circumstances, when she gets an order she must obey it cheerfully and readily, not in a slow, sullen manner. Scouts never grumble, whine, or frown. In time of danger even a smile or a song will cheer and hearten up the wavering. So keep it up all the time.

9. A Girl Scout is Cheerful

under all circumstances. When she gets an order she

should obey it cheerily and readily, not in a slow, hang-dog sort of way, and should sing even if she dislikes it.

Scouts never grumble at hardships, nor whine at each other, nor frown when put out.

A Scout goes about with a smile and singing. It cheers her and cheers other people, especially in time of danger.

10. A Girl Scout Is Thrifty

That is, she saves every penny she can and puts it into the bank so she can have money to keep herself when out of work and thus not be a burden to others, or that she may have money to give to others more needy than herself.

There are ten Girl Scout Laws, one for each finger on a Scout's hand, and the object of these laws is to make one LOYAL, KIND, CHEERFUL, and OBEDIENT.

First Camp-Fire Story

Can we find a character in American history more inspiring as an example for girls and American women than Margaret Brent of Maryland? In the autumn of 1638 she came to the colony with her two brothers. She is described as a great beauty but always in that remote and struggling community "a woman of affairs." She studied law and was the trusted adviser of the governor and founder of the colony. It seems more than probable that she was largely instrumental in shaping the wise policy that so successfully carried Maryland through the many vicissitudes of its early history. Certain it is that the treatment of the Indians was that recommended by her as well as the Toleration Act. A Catholic herself she respected the rights of all religions and brought about harmony where others would have failed. Such was Lord Calvert's firm belief in her honesty that,

HELP THEIR COUNTRY

on his death-bed, he simply said, "To you Margaret I leave all. Take all and pay all." Well may we be proud of our country when we find among its founders women such as she.

THE SECOND MEETING

Bring stuff for making flags—or red and blue pencils to cut out in paper and color the flag. Show how to cut stars by folding pieces of paper five times across at the proper angles. Teach the girls the history of the flag (see page 102). Get names entered in a book for roll call and good marks. Teach them the secret passwords and salutes. At every meeting the Captain first calls the girls to "Attention" and salutes and calls over the roll, then she should proceed to ask and the girls repeat the countersign (see page 126). Practise drawing Scout signs on walls or ground with chalk or stick (to be rubbed out afterwards). Play games if out of doors; physical exercise and drill; how to make knots, slings, and ration bags.

Out-of-door Meetings

If the meeting occurs out of doors some form of Nature study may be profitably taken up. In town Scouts may see who can first locate a doctor, druggist, mail-box, or something of that sort; carefully note distance, direction, what turns are made, etc., and what objects are seen when taking a short walk; or they can play such games as "Shop-window," "Hare and Hounds," or as a competition sketch maps of town or camp grounds.

Indoors

If the meeting takes place indoors they can play "Match-sticks" to make the fingers nimble; show how to use a marlin spike, and splicing; splice a fish line with a pin for a marlin spike; or practise "Jiu-Jitsu" or "Inventory Game" or rehearse a play.

Patrols should continue practice during the week at odd times or under their Captain. Final games or exercises can be held on Saturday afternoon.

Kim's Game

Place twenty or thirty small articles on a tray or table, or the floor and cover with a cloth—different kinds of buttons, pencils, corks, nuts, string, knives or other such small things. Make a list and have a column opposite for each player's name. Uncover for just one minute and then take each player by herself and check off the articles she can remember. The winner is the one who remembers the most.

Morgan's Game

Players run quickly to a certain bill-board or shop window where an umpire is posted to time them a minute for their observation. They then run back to headquarters and report all they can remember of the advertisements on bill-board or objects in shop window.

Scout Meets Scout

Patrols of Scouts are to approach each other from a distance. The first to give the signal that the other is in sight wins. In this game it is not fair to disguise but hiding the approach in any way is admissible. You can climb a tree, ride in any vehicle, or hide behind some slowly moving or stationary object. But be sure to keep in touch with the one who is to give the signal.

It is best that others should not know the Scouts' secret passwords, so one is given at a time in this book for those that can *search best*. You will find one in the paragraph "Reading Sign or Deduction."

HELP THEIR COUNTRY

Acting Charades

may be indoors or out. A very good one is for two or three players to act as if they wanted some special thing that is in sight. The first who discovers what this is then selects some other players to act with her.

Unprepared Plays

Relate the plot of some simple play, after which assign a part to each of several to act out. Let them confer for a short time and then act it. This develops many fine talents and is one of the most useful games for the memory, expression, and imagination.

A Scout always shakes hands when she loses a game and congratulates the winner.

Second Camp-Fire Story

The story of Annie Tilis shows how well a little girl was prepared when danger threatened both herself and her father. In the Florida war with the Seminole Indians, Annie lived with her father not far from Fort Drum. As it was possible to call to the fort at any time for assistance Mr. Tilis stayed on his place to take care of his cattle. Annie used to get up in the morning and milk the cows. When she was through she would call her father and he would come and help pen up the calves so that the cows would be sure to come back at night. One morning while Annie was milking, she saw some Indians hiding close to the fence where her father would have to pass coming out of the house, and she knew that if she called out to him they would kill her at once. One of the calves that had smelt the Indians ran out into the bushes. So Annie quietly set her milk pail down, selecting a safe place for it as if she were coming back to finish milking and went after the calf, passing very near the Indian who was nearest the house but without turning her head at all, and as soon as the bush hid her from their view she slipped into the house and her father blew his horn for the soldiers. If she had made the least outcry or even ran with the milk pail in her hand the Indians would have killed both her and her father and probably surprised the garrison at the fort. Annie and one of the Indians have both told me this story. They are very old people now.

People that live in cities are often exposed to dangers, too, that make it necessary to *be prepared*. My little friend Jane Marshall saw a burglar when she came home before her mother. He was just stepping into the pantry, so she went right by him and out by the back door, which he had left open, calling her kitten in a perfectly natural manner. As soon as she was out of the house she ran to the neighbors who telephoned the police and the burglar was caught before her mother got home.

Read in history the story of Nancy Hart and her little daughter. Though but a child her habit of prompt obedience of orders saved them both from a most horrible fate. Their house was captured by the Tories who felt so secure in finding only a defenceless woman and a little girl that they proceeded to make merry, ordering Nancy to cook them a dinner. While she was doing this they amused themselves by telling her and the child what they were going to do to them after dinner. Watching her chance Nancy seized one of their guns and called to her daughter to get another. The child at once did so and when Nancy had shot one of the Tories she found the second musket passed into her hand so promptly that it was impossible for the surviving enemies to "rush" her while unarmed.

These stories show you that self-control is very necessary in being prepared in time of danger. Some people

HELP THEIR COUNTRY

will in such cases "lose their heads," as the saying is. A Scout's training is of much benefit in all such cases. Prompt obedience is also very important in the face of danger.

"In time of peace prepare for war." Happily we now are at peace, but if a war should come and find us unprepared it would be disastrous. So the Scouts should learn as far as possible how to nurse and care for the wounded, for that will be their main share in any war that may come.

DUTIES

You will see from the general contents of this book that we work in the desired details of character building through the following subjects, which are attractive to girls.

Be Womanly

No one wants women to be soldiers. None of us like women who ape men.

An imitation diamond is not as good as a real diamond. An imitation fur coat is not as good as real fur. Girls will do no good by trying to imitate boys. You will only be a poor imitation. It is better to be a real girl such as no boy can possibly be. Everybody loves a girl who is sweet and tender and who can gently soothe those who are weary or in pain. Some girls like to do scouting, but scouting for girls is not the same kind of scouting as for boys. The chief difference is in the courses of instruction. For the boys it teaches MANLINESS, but for the girls it all tends to WOMANLINESS and enables girls the better to help in the great battle of life.

Girls need not wait for war to break out to show what heroines they can be. We have many every-day heroines whose example might be followed with advantage, and we daily hear of brave girls whose pluck we admire.

Be Strong

To carry out all the duties and work of a Scout properly a girl must be strong and healthy. It may take a little time and care to make yourself so. It means a lot of exercise, running, walking, jumping, and playing games. Sleep with your windows open summer and winter and you will never catch cold. Too soft a bed tends to make people dream which is unhealthy and weakening. Don't lay abed in the morning thinking how awful it is to have to get up. Rouse out at once and take a smart turn of some quick exercise. Have a daily bath if you can. Or at least take a good rub down with a wet towel. Learn to breathe through your nose. Breathing through the mouth makes you thirsty. And so does chewing gum.

As a Scout you will be taught how to make yourself strong by taking healthy exercise, gymnastics, and drill; plenty of open air and good wholesome food—not your sticky sweets. They ruin your teeth and spoil your appetite. Take your measurements and see how you improve month by month according to the table on page 74.

Be Handy

Know how to do many useful things. Do them in the best way, the shortest way, and in the most economical manner. Study how to put things down and take them up without looking. I saw a watchmaker take a watch to pieces and put it together again without giving scarcely a glance at his tools. He knew always where he had put a thing down and his fingers reached it without a single glance to see where it lay.

Frontier Life

Many of you that live in town may some day go out to some settlement in the wilderness. Some of you have already been there and know how necessary it is to be able to look out for yourselves and others far away from any civilized help. No farther away than Florida there are some very wild places and some of us may go to the Philippines or other distant spots. However well placed you may be now times may come when you will have to know how to milk, cook, cut wood, wash clothes, act as a nurse, or even defend your life. Many things which now are done for you will have to be done without any assistance from others. All these things you can learn as a Girl Scout.

Be Good Mothers

Some time when you are grown up and have children of your own to bring up you will have to know what food to give them, how to look after their health, how to make them strong, and how to teach them to be good, hardworking, honorable citizens in our big growing country.

Almost every man you read of in history, who has risen to a high position, has been helped by his mother. We have had many great and good men and they were made great and good by their mothers.

To be Observant

means noticing and knowing all about animals, which is gained by following up their foot tracks and other signs and creeping up to them so that you can watch them in their natural state, and learning the different kinds of animals and all their habits. You only kill animals when in want of food, for no Scout should needlessly injure any animal unless it is destructive or harmful. You will get to know them as little friends and not want to kill them. The finest sport of hunting is in the Woodcraft or tracking and hunting, not in the killing.

Besides Woodcraft includes the knowledge of how to read the meaning of signs and tracks— whether running away or just feeding about or playing. It includes the art of finding your way in the woods and wild places; what wild fruits, roots, or mushrooms are

IMPROVISED STRETCHER MADE OF STAVES AND HANDKERCHIEFS

HELP THEIR COUNTRY

fit for food and which are not; which are liked by certain birds and animals and so are likely to attract them.

Among civilized surroundings you may practise on the tracks of men, horses, vehicles, etc.; note the pace, how long since the track has been made. Dew and spider-webs are fine indications sometimes of age. A frightened bird may tell you some one is lurking near and be a means of avoiding danger.

Noticing these little "ground signs" will help in finding lost articles. By cultivating the habit of looking after small things you will observe when a strap or a bit is hurting a horse and so save him being galled or injured.

From the dress and behavior of people you may be able to see that they are up to no good and a crime even may be prevented. Possibly you may see that they are sick or in distress but too proud or brave to make a fuss about it. One of the chief duties of the Scout then is to help them.

Try to see everything. Consider it almost a disgrace if, when with others, they see anything big or small, high or low, near or far that you fail to discover. See it first if you can.

Campaigning

Scouts must, of course, be much accustomed to the open. You will be taught to put up tents and woodsman's camps for yourselves; how to build and keep up a fire and cook over it; to find the way by night or day. People learn these things in civilized communities but out in the woods they cannot "ask a policeman."

Tending the Injured

No one is ever sure that she may not meet with an accident. We hear every day of people being killed and injured on the railroad by autos or in street collisions. We will need to learn how to help in such cases. The accident may be one in which the injured are many and far from help. It is good practice to convert a camp or a club room into an improvised hospital and to try what service you can render to a bruised or maimed companion acting as the victim. Learn how to reduce a dislocation or the best way to move a person with a broken leg so as not to increase the pain or make the injury worse (see page 97).

Helping Others

Scouts cannot find a finer example to follow in history than the traditional "gentle knights" of old who went about doing good and righting wrongs. Do a good turn every day to somebody. That is one of the Scouts' rules. Tie a knot that you will have to untie every night, and before you go to sleep think who you did your good turn for that day. If you find you have forgotten or that the opportunity had not arisen that day do two next day to make up for it. By your Scouts' oath you know you are on your honor bound to do this. It need be only a small thing. Help some one across the street or show him the way he wishes to go. Aid a person overburdened with packages or pick one up that has dropped. Any little thing of this sort will count, but you must accept nothing for doing it but thanks.

Home Life

To make others happy is the Scout's first wish. When you come home from work or school turn your thoughts to those you love at home and try what you can do to lighten their burdens or cheer them through dark days. It is not beyond the power of a little girl to make home peaceful and happy. Perhaps there are little ones to think of. They are quick to copy and every good action and kind word of yours may have an effect on them through their whole lives.

Patriotism

You belong to the great United States of America, one of the great world powers for enlightenment and liberty. It did not just grow as circumstances chanced to form it. It is the work of your forefathers who spent brains and blood to complete it. Even when brothers fought they fought with the wrath of conviction, and when menaced by a foreign foe they swung into line shoulder to shoulder with no thought but for their country.

In all that you do think of your country first. We are all twigs in the same fagot, and every little girl even goes to make up some part or parcel of our great whole nation.

Part II

CAMPING

It is advisable that Patrols or Companies should have some place of their own at which to camp. Some small plot of woodland is easily secured near most any of our cities. At the beaches it is frequently impossible to secure the privacy desirable. The seaside is not easily fenced in. If you own your camping ground all desirable sanitary conditions can be looked after and buildings of a more or less permanent nature erected. Even a "brush house" in a spot which you are allowed to use exclusively is better than having to hunt a place every time you want to camp out. "Gypsying" from place to place is unadvisable.

When you have your own camp, too, much better chances for study will be found possible. You will have your own trees, flowers, and birds to notice and care for, and a record of them is valuable even in a very limited space. Think of the beautiful work of White—*The Natural History of Selbourne.*

Name your camp by all means. Long ago I formed the habit of naming all my camps using by preference the name of the first bird seen there. Now I use the Seminole name if I can remember it. So we have our "Ostata" and "Tashkoka" and I hope soon some others. Some of the names are too hard, though, for civilized tongues. "Mooganaga" for the name, might hurt somebody's mouth who tries to pronounce it.

When going into camp *never* forget matches. When leaving camp I used to put all my spare matches into a dry empty bottle, cork it tight, and hide it. After many years I have found my matches as good as "new" where

I had hidden them. By rubbing two sticks together one can make a fire without matches.

Camping out is one of my hobbies. Walks and picnics are all very well as far as they go, but to get the full benefit of actual contact with Nature it is absolutely necessary to camp out. That does not mean sleeping on wet bare ground but just living comfortably out of doors, where every breath of heaven can reach you and all wild things are in easy reach. A camp can be nicely planned within daily reach of many of our large cities but should be far enough to escape city sounds and smells. It is not a camp, however, if it is where a stream of strangers can pass by at any time of the day or night within sight and hearing.

Water is a supreme requisite at any camp. Water to swim in may be dispensed with in extreme cases but you can't carry your water with you and have a comfortable time. I have been where I had to do it so I know how it is. Also I have had to dig water out of the ground. That is not an easy operation so be sure and camp near a well or spring. Wood, too, you will want and it must be dry. Don't try to cook with fat pine. It's all right to kindle with but not for cooking. Your bacon fried over it will be as fine eating as a porous plaster. Fry your potatoes. If you must roast them dig a hole in the ashes and cover them deep. Then go away and forget them. Let some one else come along and cook all sorts of things on top of them. When you come back rake them out of the ashes and astonish every one.

Be sure your cooking fire is not too big. You must be able to get up to it comfortably close without scorching your face. Start a small fire and feed it as required with small dry twigs. Cooking over an outdoor fire is a fine art and has to be studied carefully. It should be called almost a post-graduate course in the camp studies. Of course the regular camp-fire can be made as big and smoky as you like. Smoke is fine to watch but not to breathe. Even the mosquitoes don't like it.

Roughing it is all very fine to talk about, but it is best to make your camp as comfortable as possible. The ground is nice to sleep upon but not stones and sticks. It's really astonishing how big a stick no longer than your finger can grow in one night. Take my word for it and don't try it. It won't pay. A hammock is my preference but a cot is about as good. On a pinch twigs and grass are not to be despised. Moss is apt to be moist but there is no possible objection to clean dry sand. Shake yourself well though before breakfast as sand don't mix well with the early morning meal.

Be sure not to let your fire get away from you and spread. Besides the damage to trees and fences that it may do it is impossible to tell what suffering it may cause to animal life. When you have seen helpless young birds that have been roasted in their nest, or a little struggling rabbit with its eyes burnt blind you will realize what a fire, that has been raging in the woods, can do. So again take my word for it and be very careful.

FOREST FIRES!

To prevent forest fires Congress passed the law approved May 5, 1900, which—

Forbids setting fire to the woods, and
Forbids leaving any fires unextinguished.

When you leave your camp clean up. Fragments of food—not pickles—can be put up somewhere for the birds. At some of our camps we have regular places to feed the birds and they get to know what time to come there. Here in the woods my wrens have established for themselves the hour of sunrise, and it is partly to escape the scolding I am sure to get for neglect that I am such an early bird myself. Mrs. Jenny scolds like a dollar watch being wound up but for actual singing she can beat any bird in the woods.

Perhaps you notice that I have said nothing about snakes. Now it is really a very rare thing for me to see a snake in the woods. You have to look very carefully to find them, for they seem to be about the most timid of all creatures. So far as danger from poisonous snakes is concerned you are in much more danger from the driver of a dray than from a snake. I have been run over by a dray but never bitten by a snake. Take my word for it, snakes are much more afraid of you than you are of them. Give them the least little bit of a chance and they will be out of the way before you can see them. A gorged snake—that is one that has just taken a full meal—may be sluggish but in a majority of cases he will crawl away and hide in some secure place till the process of digestion is over. Do not go near a tub if you are afraid of water for you can get drowned in it about as easy as you can get bitten by a snake in the woods. And to wind the subject up not one-tenth of the people who get snake bite, die from it. A very few do die but most of them die from the bad treatment they receive afterwards. The "deadly auto" will not get out of your way but all snakes will.

Once in a while you may find clinging in a low bush a pretty little green snake. It will readily submit to being handled and is perfectly harmless. I have found these snakes useful in the house to kill flies. The harmless snakes are the brown snake, the common banded moccasin, the black mountain snake, the green snake, and the garter and ring-necked snakes wear Eve's wedding-ring as a collar. They cannot hurt and they eat up quantities of insects, but beware of the yellow and brown rattlesnakes, especially after rainy weather, for it is said that after wet weather they cannot make any noise with their rattles and therefore you are not warned of their approach. The most deadly snake, the moccasin, is brownish with a flat head.

The green lizards, too, will almost rid a house of flies if left to wander about at will. I always bring one in if I find it and it gets to be quite tame. The fence lizard, a scaly alligator looking chap, is just as useful but never gets tame.

Try petting a toad some time. He will get to be quite at home in a garden and pay well, for he will eat all kinds of destructive insects. Some gardeners buy toads paying as high as a quarter apiece for they know how much good they can do. A toad digs his hole backwards. Watch him and see the fun. In the spring if there is water near he may be induced to sing to you. If you think he is slow and clumsy you have only to see how quick he can catch a fly.

Provisioning a Camp

This should be a matter of mature consideration. Unless there is some place near by where deficiencies can be supplied your camp may be a misery instead of a pleasure. Have lists made out of the things each is to bring, if it is to be a coöperative affair. It may be best to have a committee even, if it is a committee of one, to do all the buying. But even in this case individual tastes must be consulted. A full list should be made out and strictly adhered to. At one camp where each brought what she thought best there were six cans of soup, four pounds of sugar, and no tea or coffee.

Canned goods are all very well if you do not have to carry them too far. So too are potatoes. For lightness on long trips, dried fruits and meal or grits are a wise selection. Oatmeal is light and easy to cook. Prepared batter-cake flour is a pure joy to the camp cook. Once when camping in the mountains we had unexpected difficulties. We were at such an elevation that water boiled at too low a temperature to cook many things "done," so the frying-pan there reigned supreme. As

HELP THEIR COUNTRY

to that same frying pan be sure to select the "long tailed breed." If not you will have to splice out the handle with a long stick. Never pack up your "unwetables" in paper bags. At any time a shower or even a heavy dew at night may make you run short on salt, sugar, or flour. Covered tin cans are too cheap to make it necessary to run any such risks. Have a lantern and oil of course. Candles blow out too easily to be of much use. For sudden calls for a light the pocket electric affair is very good and cheap. Keep it standing up. The batteries waste pretty fast if it is left down on the side.

As to the quantity of provisions to be taken that depends of course on the length of stay. Consult any good military or naval ration list and a very good guess can be made. They all seem to lay stress on beans which certainly are very good if you have the "Boston" appetite.

Keep your camp clean. Keep it in order. Let your motto be, "Tidy as you go." It is as bad to have to hunt for a thing you want in camp as it is at home and particularly exasperating if when you have found it you must wash it before using. "A place for everything and that place anywhere" is a bad camp rule, though it does sound as if it was a real easy way of disposing of the matter. Dig a hole to throw slops in and do not let them "fly" on the ground. You may want to sit down right there. Whatever the birds will eat should be put aside for them. All other scraps and things that may become offensive *must* be buried. Don't start to breed flies or fever. When near the water some part of this rule may be dispensed with in favor of the fish and crabs. They may be judiciously baited up, but if you are going to fish for them see that they are not overfed.

There are times and seasons when wild fruits and berries are a most welcome addition to the camp fare, but unless you are perfectly sure of the supply do not reckon on them too much in making up your provision

Semaphore Useful in Camping.

COOKING IN THE OPEN.

list. Better let them be a sort of joyful surprise. So too of fish and game. "Don't count your chickens before they are hatched." Fresh smilax shoots can scarcely be told from asparagus. Palmetto cabbage well cooked is fine; poorly prepared it is vile. Let some one that knows about these things "do" them for you.

The "gipsy kettle" is picturesque and only picturesque. Drive two stout crotched stakes each side of the fire and put a stout stick across them. Use strong wire hooks—S-shaped on which to hang pots over the fire. If hung through the handle on the stick they are apt to boil over and put out the fire before you know it. They can be quickly lifted from the wire hooks as soon as they begin to look dangerous. Even the coffee pot can be rigged with a wire handle by which to be hung. Wire and string are my special hobbies in camp. Fan a fire instead of blowing it. Your breath has lost most of its combustible gas. A tin or wooden plate makes a good fan. Put away dry kindling every night. You don't know what sort of weather it will be to-morrow.

Use all precaution against your fire spreading. This is particularly necessary where there are tents. A dry tent will almost "whisk" up in smoke if the fire catches it. Rake dry leaves well away from about the fire. It may be best sometimes to make "a burn" round the camp. Do this a little at a time beating out all traces of the fire in the part burnt over. Be in no hurry about this but be thorough. Leave no smouldering embers or chunks of rotten wood smoking behind you. Burn clean as you go.

Daily Routine in Camp

Have a set of general orders posted every morning. There should be one officer of the day and one orderly. These will be appointed in turn. The general order should be read before breakfast and include all duties and so far as possible the excursions and games for the day. In appointing cooks and details for the various duties be sure not to work the "willing horse" too hard but let all share as much alike as possible. Some will always want to volunteer too often and some will try to avoid certain duties distasteful to themselves or "swap" with others. This should not be allowed but helping must never be barred completely. Inspect camp personally at least once a day and call attention to shortcomings kindly without chiding. You can help your girls to help themselves. A "driver" in camp is sure to breed hard feelings and cause discontent. The camp is a hard school for the instructor. The only necessary law in a camp is that after lights are out at night, no one must speak. Silence should reign.

In some places mosquitoes are very troublesome. Oil of citronella will drive them away for a time but a "smudge" may be necessary. They won't stay in smoke or wind, so hunt the breeze. There are some other flies just as bad to which the same treatment may be applied. "Black-flies" of the northern woods are about the worst insect pest in America, though the mosquitoes in some parts of the South are nearly as bad. In some of the coast regions, too, there is a species of "sandfly" or midge that is exceedingly annoying, but all of these are readily controlled by the "smudge." This is a steady smoke not necessarily of an ill-smelling nature. One of the very best materials for a "smudge" is green cedar branches. They need some pretty hot coals to keep them smouldering but are very effective.

Very few accidents need happen in camp. But still it may be a wise precaution to go over with each patrol, before the camping trip, some simple exercise in bandaging and other "First Aid" exercises. In a book of the scope of this one it is not possible to give a full course of instruction in such matters, so it seems best to make only

HELP THEIR COUNTRY

casual mention and leave details to the judgment of the Patrol leaders.

If any boating is to be a part of the programme they should inform themselves carefully which of their patrol can swim and just how expert they are. Also instruct in methods of throwing things to a drowning person or one who has just met with some mishap in a boat—such for instance as losing an oar. A board or a plank should not be thrown toward a person in the water but launched toward them. When adrift in an unmanageable boat cast anchor and wait for assistance. *Never rock a boat for fun.* A Scout who so far forgets herself as to do such a foolhardy act should be forbidden to go into a boat again for some time as a punishment. Most drowning accidents are from some such *fun*. It is *sin*—not *fun*.

When bathing obey strictly all orders regarding distance to be ventured and other rules. You may think they are mere summary restrictions but you are probably not the best judge.

Last summer a party of boys were bathing. Contrary to orders they scattered apart instead of keeping close together. While the Captain's back was turned looking after the smaller boys, some of the big boys began to dare each other to go farther and farther out. When the Captain blew the whistle for them some still persisted in swimming away from the beach and one of them was drowned. And to make it still worse he drowned in shallow water where, if he had only known or had kept his wits about him, he could have waded ashore.

Hints to Instructors

Camp Orders

In going into camp it is essential to have a few "Standing Orders" published, which can be added to from time to time, if necessary. These should be carefully explained to patrol leaders, who should then be held fully responsible for their Scouts carrying them out exactly.

Such orders might point out that each patrol will camp separately from the others, and that there will be a comparison between the respective cleanliness and good order of tents and surrounding ground.

Patrol leaders to report on the good work or otherwise of their Scouts, which will be recorded in the Captain's book of marks.

Bathing under strict supervision to prevent non-swimmers getting into dangerous water. No girl must bathe when not well.

Bathing picket of two good swimmers will be on duty while bathing is going on, and ready to help any girl in distress. This picket will be in the boat (undressed) with bathing costume and overcoat on. They may only bathe when the general bathing is over and the last of the bathers has left the water. If bathing in the surf, a stake should be driven into the sand on the beach and a rope securely fastened to the stake so that non-swimmers can hold on to the rope in the water.

Orders as to what is to be done in case of fire alarm.

Orders as to boundaries, grounds to be worked over, damages to fences, property, good drinking water, etc.

No Scout allowed out of bounds without leave.

No lads allowed inside bounds without leave.

Camping Equipment Necessary for One Week or Longer

1 Transport wagon.
2 Tents for girls.
1 Tent for officer.
3 Mallets and sufficient tent-pegs.
2 Blankets for each Scout.
2 Blankets for officer.
1 **Kit bag each (2 ft. by 1 ft. or bigger).**

HELP THEIR COUNTRY

8 Waterproof ground sheets.
3 Buckets.
3 Hurricane lamps.
2 Balls of twine (medium).
1 Spade.

Kitchen Equipment

Saucepan or stew-pan or regulation billy.
Large frying pan.
Large kettle.
Gridiron.
Butcher's knife.
Kitchen fork.
Ladle.
Tea strainer.
Three tea cloths.
Cleaning rags.

Clothing for Each Girl Scout

Old coat or waterproof or cape.
2 Woolen vests.
2 Pair woolen stockings.
1 Flannel night-dress or sleeping suit.
1 Pair stout walking shoes or boots.
1 Pair canvas shoes.
1 Sweater or old jacket.
1 Bathing dress.
2 Handkerchiefs.
2 Towels.
Hairbrush and comb.
Toothbrush.
Soap.

Personal Equipment for Each Scout

Haversack.
Billy or mess tin.

Girl Scout staff.
Knife and fork.
Spoon and teaspoon.
Cup and saucer.
Plate.
Safety matches.
Whistle.
Three linen ration bags.
Small pocket note-book.
Pencil.
General "Hussif," fitted with needles, thread, scissors, and thimble.

Useful Knots

Every one should be able to tie knots. A knowledge of knots is useful in every trade or calling, and forms an important part of a Girl Scout's training.

As it may happen some day that a life may depend on a knot being properly tied you ought to know the proper way to do so.

THE BOWLINE is a loop that will not slip after the first grip. First make a loop, then pass the end up through it, round the back of the standing part, and down through the loop again. It is often used as a halter for horses.

THE RUNNING BOWLINE. This is the nautical slip knot. First make the loop as in the ordinary bowline but allow a good length of end (A). Pass it round the standing part and up through the loop, and continue as in the ordinary bowline.

THE REEF KNOT. It is used to join two dry ropes of the same thickness, will not slip, and can easily be untied when wanted. Do not confuse it with the "Granny" knot. It is the *only* knot used in First Aid work.

THE CLOVE HITCH is made with two half-hitches. When fastened to a pole and pulled tight it can neither slip up nor down. Greatly used in pioneering work

HELP THEIR COUNTRY

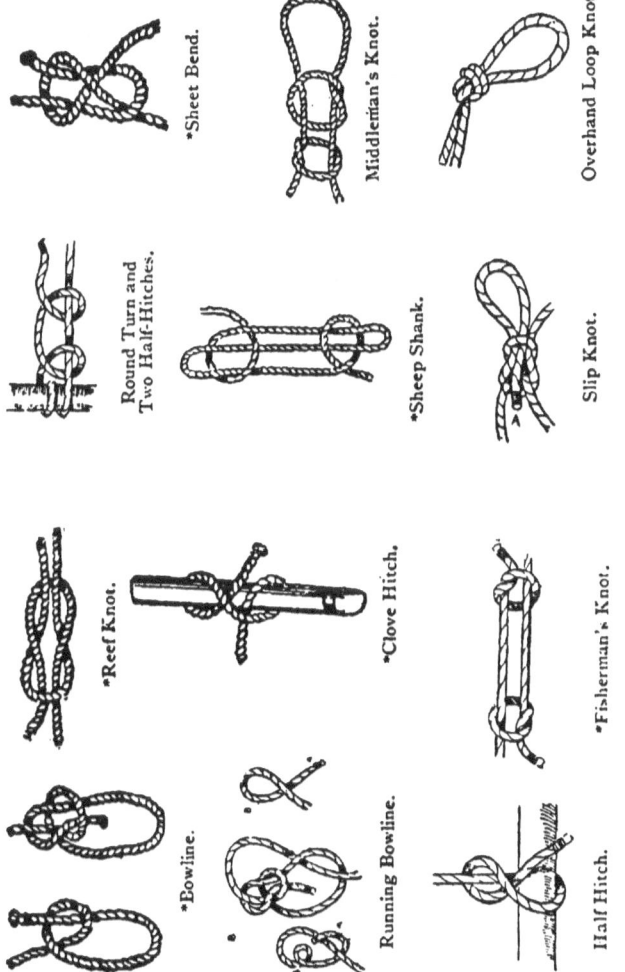

The Half-Hitch. Pass the end round a pole, then round the standing part, then through below itself again.

The Fisherman's Knot. Make this knot by tying a simple knot on rope B with the end of rope A, then tie a similar knot on rope A with the end of rope B. Pull the standing parts and the knots will remain fast.

Round Turn and Two Half-Hitches. It is use for making fast a rope so that the strain will not jamb hitches.

The Sheet Bend. Used for uniting two dry ropes of different thicknesses. First form a loop, then pass the end of the other rope up through the loop, round the back of the end and standing part of loop, and through below itself.

The Sheep-Shank. A Scout should never cut rope unless absolutely necessary. To shorten a guy rope on tent or marquee, gather the rope in the form of two long loops and pass a half-hitch over each loop. It remains firm under a good strain and can be easily undone when required.

Middleman's Knot. Somewhat similar to the fisherman's knot but in this case only one rope is used. Can safely be used as a halter.

The Slip Knot. You sometimes want to release a knot quickly so this knot is used. It is simply the reef knot with one of the ends (A) pushed through one of the loops. To release, pull end A.

Overhand Loop Knot. When pulling a rope you may wish to gain more purchase on it or you may wish to insert a short stick to pull with. Use the loop knot shown in our diagram.

Important. Many of the knots shown on these pages are open so that you may more easily see their working, but when in use they should always be drawn taut.

OPEN-AIR PURSUITS

INSTRUCTION in the art of observation and deduction cannot be laid down by any fixed set of rules. Practice is the main thing, but there are some few points that can be well learned from simple common-sense. It is, for instance, needless to try to smoke a rabbit out of a hollow if there are old spider-webs across it. But if there is fresh mud there you may find either a coon or a swamp rabbit—not "Molly Cotton-tail" rabbit for she hates dirty toes.

Children are proverbially quick observers, for everything is new to them and first impressions are strongest. As they grow, the interest must be kept up, and if it extends into their riper years it will probably last through life. Just here is one of the very best things about a Scout's training. It is extending first impressions past the receptive age into the deductive and argumentative stage of the mentality. So, my dear instructors, make it so interesting that it may become habitual and fairly grafted on the character.

Stalking

"Sign" is a term that covers a multitude of small things. It is in the interpretation of "sign" that some of the very finest work of the human mind comes in. Preconcerted signs or signals have been used from the remotest times and are to day the only means of communication between savages. Some of their signs seem to be past finding out. When Geronimo was taken to St. Augustine it was known to the Seminoles in the Everglades ten days before the news reached the white inhabitants of the frontier. To this day no one knows how they found out that the "bad Indian" was there. "Ista-chatta holwagas St. Augustine" was all we could get out of them. A few of their signs are known and their fireplace sign is worth learning. Three burnt sticks are placed at the last camp-fire to tell the direction they have gone from this spot. Two of them always make a V point and if the third is laid at the point of the V̲ it means north. Across the open end of the V⁻ it means south. At one side | V it means east and V | would mean west. Now the above mark as I have made it for south would really mean southwest, as the stick which indicates direction is a little way to the west side. Northwest would be V.

V̲ North
V⁻ South
|V East
V| West
V_ Northwest

But "sign" as studied by the Scouts deals mostly with small natural bits of information likely to escape any but specially trained eyes and senses. For do not imagine that "signs" are always to be seen. They are to be smelt. My first bit of detective work was done through smelling one of my uncle's cigars which led to the arrest of a burglar. And that was the first intimation we had that our house had been entered. With sounds, too, we often have to deal. The frightened cry of a bird may be as good a warning to you of danger as the bark of a watch-dog. The sticky feeling of the pantry door-knob may convict your little brother of stealing jam. Probably all of us have some peculiar way of remembering direction and places.

The signs that are at the right height to catch the eye pay the best. A good big sign "Dressmaking" when hung above the door had never attracted a customer. Brought down beside the door it brought in two customers the first day. So to see everything don't look in the easiest place or the usual place. Glance at the ground and then up photographing as it were on

HELP THEIR COUNTRY 35

your memory the things you see. Look back when walking to see how things will look if you come back that way. Make a mark in the woods if necessary by twisting a twig. In the open a knot may be tied in the grass. If going out in a boat always look back so there will be no doubt as to which landing or wharf to come back to. A deer pressed by the dogs will swim out to sea. The quick turn of the birds flying over him will tell you just where he is. Find the track where he went in and before night he will come ashore just about there, for before he went in he took his bearings so as to know where to come back.

DETAILS OF PEOPLE. It is very instructive to note the different people we meet and try to form estimates of their character and disposition by their looks and clothes. A priest once told me it was easy to tell a Church of England clergyman because he was always just a shade too clean. And it seems impossible to lose the effect of military drill. Old soldiers intuitively know each other. Rich and poor are hard to tell apart in America by their dress but the speech often gives a fine clue. But I can tell you one thing as to shoes that if you practise scouting much in the woods it will lead to a great saving in shoes. It soon becomes instinctive to step lightly.

CULTIVATE THE FACULTY OF REMEMBERING TIME. Some people can say a thing happened on a certain day but do not know the hour even approximately. When I am in the city and hear any fire alarm I am sure to notice the time. It may some time be good evidence. One of my most highly prized possessions is a full set of observations on the Charleston earthquake. It is the only complete set ever taken and I never got paid for it except in promises.

If you bear a very simple fact in mind you can tell the distance of a thunder-storm. There are 365 days in a year. That is also the number of yards sound goes in a second—or near enough for all practical purposes—or you may say if you choose five seconds to go a mile. Noting the elapsed time between the lightning and the thunder a moment's calculation will enable you to make a fairly good estimate.

Games

INVENTORY GAME. Let each girl go into a room for half a minute and when she comes out let her make a list of what she has seen. Then compare lists to find who has seen the most.

TESTING NOSES. This is easiest with the competitors blindfolded. Let them smell different things and tell what they are. Also the objects may be placed in bags but this means much more work.

CHASING AN OWL. Another good stalking game is chasing the owl. This is done in thick woods where one Guide represents the owl hooting at intervals and then moving to one side for a distance. Each pursuer when seen is called out of the game and the owl, if a real good one, may get safely back to her stump.

TURKEY AND WILDCAT is played by the turkey blindfolded "going to roost" in some place where there are plenty of twigs or dry leaves to crack and rustle. At the first sound the turkey jumps. If not then in reach of the wildcat she is safe and another wildcat has a chance. This is sometimes very laughable for the turkey being blindfolded may jump right on the wildcat.

FAR AND NEAR. On any walk, preferably in patrol formation, let each keep a list of things seen such as birds, flowers, different kinds of trees, insects, vehicles, tracks, or other "sign." Score up in points at the end of the walk on return to the club rooms.

TRACKING

This is also called "spooring." One of the best ways to learn tracking is to begin with the tracks of

BASKET-BALL AND TENNIS PLAYERS.

HOW GIRLS CAN

NUMERALS

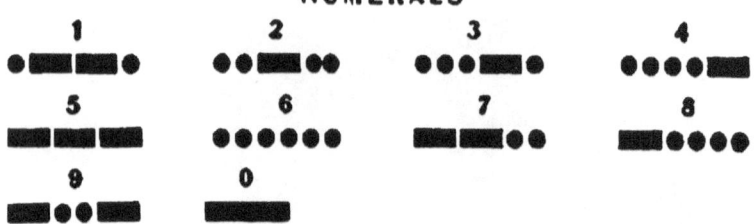

Punctuation

Comma, ● ■ ● ■	Exclamation, ■ ■ ■
Semicolon, Si	Parenthesis, Pn
Colon, Ko	Brackets, Bn
Period, ● ● ■ ■ ● ●	Dollar mark, Sx
Interrogation, ■ ● ● ■ ●	Dash, Dx
Quotation, Qn	Hyphen, Hx
Paragraph, ■ ■ ■ ■	Underline, Ux

Signals

4. Start me.
5. Have you anything for me?
9. Train order (or important military message) — give away.
13. Do you understand?

All sorts of changes can be made when the signals are committed to memory. Flags—up for a dot and side for a dash is one of the commonest and easiest for the beginner; or whistles—long and short blasts. Even the hand or a hat can be substituted; coughing, stamping, and scratching with the foot or a bit of stick. In fact endless changes can be invented for use with this Code.

COMMANDS AND SIGNALS

For the use of the Girl Scouts the following list of words of Command and Whistle Signals has been compiled.

Commands

"Fall in" (in line).
"Alert" (stand up smartly).
"Easy" (stand at case).
"Sit easy" (sit or lie in ranks).
"Dismiss" (break off).
"Right" or "Left" (turn accordingly).
"Patrol right or patrol left" (patrol in line wheels).
"Quick march" (step off with the left foot first).
"Double" (run with arms down).
"Scouts' pace" (walk fifty paces and run fifty paces alternately).

Whistle Signals

1. One long blast means "Silence," "Alert," Listen for next signal.
2. A succession of long slow blasts means "Go out," "Get farther away," or "Advance," "Extend," "Scatter."
3. A succession of quick short blasts means "Rally," "Close in," "Come together," "Fall in."
4. Alternate short and long blasts mean "Alarm," "Look out," "Be ready," "Man your alarm posts."
5. Three short blasts followed by one long one from the Captain calls up the patrol leaders.

Any whistle signal must be instantly obeyed at the double as fast as you can run, regardless of anything you may be doing.

By previous agreement many other signals may be arranged. It all depends on the exigencies to be met or the special order or informations to be conveyed. But these few dominant signals should be strictly adhered to in all drills and exercises of Scouts. The compiler of the present volume thinks it unwise to print the secret words so they are left for the patrol leaders and Captain to communicate verbally.

Hand Signals

"Advance" "Forward"	Swing the arm from rear to front, below the shoulder.
"Retire"	Circle the arm above the head.
"Halt"	Raise the arm to full extent above head.
"Double"	The closed fist moved up and down between your shoulder and thigh.
"Quick time"	To change from the "Double" to the "Quick Time," raise the hand to the shoulder.
"Reinforce"	Swing the arm from the rear to the front above the shoulder.
"Lie down"	With the open hand make two or three slight movements towards the ground.
"Wheel"	Extend your arm in line with your shoulder and make a circular movement in the direction required.
"Incline"	Extend your arm in line with your shoulder and make a turn with your body in the direction required.

HELP THEIR COUNTRY

Scout Signs.

Sign.	Secret Patrol or Troop Sign.	Meaning.
→		Road to be followed.
▭→		Letter hidden 3 paces from here in direction of arrow.
✕		This path not to be followed.
⊙		"I have gone home."
⟩⟩⟨		War or trouble about.
⟩⟩⟩		Peace.
🪨		We camped here because one of us was sick.
⊖→		A long way to good water, go in direction of arrow.
⊖↓		Good water not far in this direction.
⊖		This is good water.
🦊 4 G W.		Signature of Scout No. 4 of the Fox Patrol, 21st Glasgow.

Shaking a blanket: I want to talk to you.
Hold up a tree-branch: I want to make peace.
Hold up a weapon (axe) means war: I am ready to fight.
Hold up a pole horizontally, with hands on it: I have found something.

Self-Defence

SHOOTING

All Scouts should know how to shoot. By this I do not mean that you should go all day behind some big dog and try to kill the birds he finds for you, for that is the most useless form of shooting, all things considered, that can be devised. What I mean is that Scouts should know how to load and fire a gun or other firearm so as not to be at a loss for a means of defense should an emergency arise. It is one of the best means to "be prepared." My preference for practice of this kind is a small rifle as being much less dangerous than any form of pistol and excellent training for hand and eye. Avoid, however, the very high power modern firearms—that kind that "shoot to-day and kill next week," as there is too much danger of reaching some one that is out of sight. The same may be said of the automatic pistol which fills too large a circle with missiles of sudden death.

Archery

The bows and arrows of our ancestors are not to be despised as a means of training hand and eye. Archery is excellent practice for the eye, and good exercise for the muscles. It makes no noise, does not disturb game or warn the enemy. Scouts should know how to shoot with bows and arrows, and can make them for themselves. The arrow, twenty-six inches long, must be as "straight as an arrow" and tipped with a heavy head, with wings to keep it level. Ash wood is the best. The bow should be unstrung when not in use, or it will get bent. It is usually made your own height. Old gloves should be worn.

How to Secure a Burglar with Eight Inches of Cord

Make a slip-knot at each end of your cord. Tie the burglar's hands behind him by passing each loop over his little fingers. Place him face downwards, and bend his knees. Pass both feet under the string, and he will be unable to get away.

The Secret Despatch

The Captain goes on ahead to hide, leaving two secret orders for two patrols (or more).

HELP THEIR COUNTRY

Written outside is a different place for each to go to. When each patrol has arrived at that place they may open the secret orders. There they will find further directions to go to a certain place where the Captain is to be found. She times which gets there first. Notice which way the wind is blowing, in case she directs you to go by the wind, and know where the north is, as she may order to a point of the compass or by Scout signs, see page 41.

CIRCUS GAME

Players take characters, such as the ringmaster, the clown, the horses, performing dogs, monkeys, acrobats. Lay down staves to mark the ring. No laughing permitted without paying a forfeit.

The clowns do all they can to make the acrobats laugh, but must not touch the performers, or they pay a forfeit. The master and clown hold hoops for the others to jump through. Small monkeys or dogs can ride on horses' backs.

EMPRESS EUGÉNIE'S CIRCLE

(A Good Method of Sitting down to Rest when the Ground is Wet.)

The Empress Eugénie's account of how the Austrian soldiers keep dry when resting:

Walk round in a circle and form a ring of about eighteen or twenty persons standing, behind one another, each one with her hands on the next one's shoulders. At a given signal all sit down at once on the knees of the person next behind them. All must wait for the signal to rise.

Provided they all do it at the signal it is quite safe, and the girls can in this way rest themselves, even if the ground is very wet. Staves may be used in the outside hand.

Place the tallest girls on one side, and the smallest opposite, and the rest according to height so that a big girl has a fairly strong girl to rest on.

WOODCRAFT

HINTS to instructors how to teach natural history. Take your Scouts into the country by all means. If this is impossible show them the animals in a zoo or even a museum of natural history. Let them learn how to harness a horse or milk a cow; how a horse or a cow lies down and gets up. Many children who have seen them all their lives cannot describe the motions. Learn to milk and care for the milk; to churn and make butter.

Studying animals and plants teaches the value of little things. We have to take pains to learn all the small though important details. Learn to move quietly; to feel with your feet without looking away from the bird or animal you are watching. This is so as not to crack a stick. Wild things do not mind talking in low tones half as much as the sharp snap of a twig. Never try to peep from behind a tree, bring the body slowly from behind it all at once, and never give the head a quick jerk in any direction. You can learn to twist your eyes and then bring the head slowly round. If discovered try to sway down slowly like a bending branch. Dropping with a jerk is a fruitful source of alarm.

In Florida I have seen a Seminole walk up to within shot of a deer in the open prairie. While feeding a deer holds his tail down. When about to raise his head he flicks it a little sideways. If anything excites his suspicion he sets his ears forward and holds them still. When he is satisfied that there is no danger down goes his tail first and then his head. That is the time to make a nearer approach. Even when watchful I have seen my Indian allay their fears and even cause them to approach him by stooping low in the grass and flicking a white rag behind him in imitation of a deer walking along and look-

HOW GIRLS CAN HELP THEIR COUNTRY 45

ing for a place to lie down. Imitating this will make a very good game of STALKING THE DEER.

But all this woodcraft and play will fall flat and totally fail of accomplishing any permanent success if we fail to study nature systematically. The best time is early in the morning. All things are fresh then and the more active birds and animals on the move. Take a position by some running water or a spring where they like to wash and drink and by keeping perfectly still you may get very intimate with the ways some of them make their toilet. Each has its own peculiar way of taking the morning bath and very pretty pictures may be got of little birds throwing off the dripping water. Here is where a good camera pays. If it is a mere "snap-shot" affair that you have remember that you must catch your little sitter when a beam of sunshine is full upon him.

There are, too, things of the night well worth study. It is too bad that there is such a senseless prejudice against the night air, and the more so as the most prejudiced people are those that too often turn night into day with their late fashionable hours. Among the Seminoles there is a very pretty belief that the dead—or as they say "those that sleep"—are fond of coming back to earth in the night, and visiting their living friends. A very small Seminole child selects the night time to travel to the camp alone, for he will tell you, "Those that sleep are with me now."

That same little boy told me a very pretty story about Yohiska, the Bluebird who, when the birds tried which could fly the highest, hid on the back of Hadkitikfunga, the great Eagle, and actually mounted a little higher than the latter did after his soaring flight had exhausted him. In proof of this the bluebird still wears some of the blue which he then rubbed from the top of the sky.

But the night, though at times perfectly enchanting, cannot for genuine enjoyment compare with the sweet morning hours. See the sun rise as often as you can. I very seldom miss it. It is the daintiest bit of the day.

Most people sleep too much. They sleep at the wrong end of the night. It was a superstition in bygone days that the morning air was unhealthy and that all kinds of sickness lurked in the evening mists. So children were called into the house at sunset and kept in bed till late in the morning. That is now known to be all a mistake. Don't go to extremes either way. I once knew a boy who wanted to sit up all night for fear something would happen and he not know it. It is better to get up and see the morning star rise than to sit up and see it. Very late so-called "fashionable" hours will undermine all but the very strongest constitutions. In very few cases is it necessary to go to sleep "with the chickens" but go to bed before midnight. Then you will be ready to rise before the sun except perhaps in midsummer. There is a peculiar charm about the morning in the open woods that must be felt to be appreciated. The trees stand black against the sky which gradually changes its color from dull gray to pink and on through gradual indescribable tints of rose red and orange till the sun gets its edge up in sight. At other times there are wonderful arches and streaks of clouds frequently throwing reflections away over into the west. The skies of morning being unmasked by the fogs and by the dust that collects in the air during the heat of the day are the most gorgeous in their coloring and increase instead of diminishing in brilliancy from minute to minute.

There are sounds, too, to enjoy in these morning hours. The herons, returning from their fishing, seem to be talking things over to each other as they go by to their roost. And they in turn seem to wake up the wild ducks who answer them from down below. Of the wood birds my earliest are a pair of quaint little brown wrens that call for their breakfast while the light is yet only gray and hop about my feet and in and out of the wood-pile

HELP THEIR COUNTRY

before they get ready to go scouting about in the bushes. Of course I have taught them this, and though every one can't have wrens there are always some birds that can be "gentled" if you will have patience with them. Perhaps the big horned owls have a little conversation before it gets too light as if making arrangements for their next hunt, and soon the crows go streaming high overhead warning each other occasionally if they spy any dangerous looking spot below. Then one by one each little bird starts up a song till there is a confused medley of a concert going on too sweet to be described in lame words. Those morning hours are a bad thing to miss.

Resident birds are those that may be found at all seasons of the year—not necessarily the same individuals. Some of them are bob-white, crows (there are two species), ruffed grouse (also called pheasant and partridge), blue jay, chickadees, nuthatches, woodpeckers, hawks, and owls. Sparrows—real wild ones of different kinds—are found at different seasons.

Migrants are birds that pass through in spring and fall to and from more remote resting places. On still nights the flocks may be heard chirping as they pass overhead as if talking to and directing or encouraging each other. Once in a while some of them may be identified by their voices but this is not the rule. Not all perform their migration in the night. The wedges of wild geese are in some parts of the country a common sight but the smaller birds seem to prefer darkness for their journey. Warblers, thrushes, and flycatchers are some of these. The complete list is very long.

Summer visitors are those that come from the South to nest and go back for the winter. Herons, rails, swallows, orioles, vireos, and tanagers may be mentioned, but this list, too, is far too long to be made complete. They with our resident species will be our most interesting acquaintances, for many of them can be "gentled" if not tamed on a very short set of lessons. Most any mother bird may be induced to feed her young under observation if proper precautions for concealment are taken.

There are winter visitors, too, to get acquainted with that come to us in very cold snaps or when their food is hidden from them by snows in the North. Some are pretty regular in their coming while others are of only casual occurrence. They are just as liable to turn up in the towns as in the country, for they are hungry little waifs and some of them are starved into tameness and so are easily studied at close range. Pine grosbeaks and redpolls will sometimes almost submit to be handled. Some others are the snow-birds and kinglets, crossbills and the rarer owls, gulls and ducks along the coast and rivers, and perhaps a shrike or two lending their aid to rid us of English sparrows. Sometimes, too, the country birds slip into town in the winter and it behooves us to keep a sharp lookout for these little strangers.

Some of the very best work a Scout can do is to get a speaking acquaintance with as many birds as possible. Have some real pets—outdoor pets among them—and feed and care for them every day. I do. I would feel badly all day if I neglected my wrens in the morning, and sometimes there are three or four other species of birds with them. One of my friends has educated his birds so that they know the time of day and at half-past eleven they call to be fed. If he neglects them for any cause they seem to get real peevish about it and raise a fuss till he comes out.

Get to know by sight and sound as many birds as you can. Jot down in your note-book the dates of arrival and also "last seen" of all the summer and winter visitors. It is valuable information for the Biological Survey at Washington and they will furnish blanks and return envelopes to all who are willing to assist them in making observations. Above all learn to protect the birds and

HELP THEIR COUNTRY

encourage others to do the same. Discourage small boys—and boys of larger growth too—from shooting and frightening them or disturbing their nests. Not that real valuable scientific collections should not be made but only those who are really competent should attempt it. Beginners must of course begin some time but it should only be after some years of close study and observation and then in such a way as to do the least possible harm.

Insects

always seem to be the dominant chord in the harmony of Nature. Birds are the chorus and flowers the rhythm. Study insects alive. Feed and raise caterpillars. Taking care of a baby caterpillar is much like taking care of any other baby. He must be handled very gently and his food carefully selected. He never cries and when he does at last go to sleep he makes his own cradle. You must then watch and see if you can catch him waking up. That is glory enough for one day. You can watch him dry his wings and take his first flight, for your baby caterpillar will be a butterfly. If you do see him take his first meal in his new state of existence you will be surprised at the length of his tongue. And the way he holds his tongue is a lesson to little chatterboxes. For he just rolls it up and tucks it away and says nothing.

Flies, bees, grasshoppers, and beetles are a study to be followed after the butterflies. Fire-flies are not flies at all but a kind of beetle. And their right Latin name—*Lamperidæ*—seems very suggestive of their accomplishments. Watch the spiders build their webs. Some of them can dive and some can fly. You doubt it. Watch them. Seeing is believing.

Shells

When people go to the beach and pick up shells they

seldom if ever do so with any motive of study or finding out anything about them but merely to take away something pretty with them. Shells really are skeletons of little soft animals. The shell grows as the animal grows as can often be seen by the rings of the substance of which it is composed. The actual formation of the shell is one of the miracles of Nature of which we as yet know really very little.

Shells may be roughly classed as single and double. All of the double shells are rights and lefts but it is difficult for any one but an expert to tell which is which. Of the single shells most of them are twisted and the same kind always twists in the same direction. A few are found that are smooth all over. In these species the animal when alive was capable of stretching himself out over the whole surface and so kept it polished. All these single shells are capable of motion but it is very slow as they have only one foot which swells and contracts in order to move them along. Some of these creatures are vegetarians while others are flesh eaters—even in many cases cannibals. Perhaps the simplest way for the beginner is to divide them into Snails, Conchs, Cones, and Limpets. Unfortunately there is no good elementary book on shells but one of my boys has found out much about them from the pictures in the dictionary.

Double shells may be classed as either Oysters, Clams, or Mussels. Oysters except when in their infancy never move about. Clams can move slowly and the mussels are always anchored by tough bundles of fibers. The oysters cannot even put their heads out doors they are such stay-at-home folks, but clams and mussels are capable of protruding quite a considerable part of their bodies. They are, however, very sensitive about being interviewed and can jump back and shut the door with almost a slam at the first appearance of danger.

Some of the shells if found with living animals in them

HELP THEIR COUNTRY

can be put into water and will walk around and even perhaps eat a little.

Fishes

are best studied in aquariums not globes. Fish globes are mere ornaments. The plants and snails and some little water insects will form a weird little world all to themselves. Speaking generally of fish, birds, or other wild things kept as pets, it is often a boon to them to be fed and cared for, they have so many enemies in their natural surroundings. My old black fox squirrel "Tar Baby" who had a broken leg would have soon died but being carefully nursed he is now as well as ever and enjoys his cage, and the tops of the tall pine trees no longer have any charm for him. He is as domestic as a kitten. Our wild pigeons might still have been preserved to us if some more people had taken the pains to keep a few as pets. Our big clumsy buffaloes—no bisons I should have said—are now being petted. Let not your minds be troubled about keeping pets. Don't drag them round with a string but just study their wants and make them happy.

The camera is a great help in Nature study. Even the little "snap-shot" affair is not to be despised, but a real camera with plates that can take pictures close to is of course the best and just as cheap. If you have not got one use the other. The best housekeepers began with mud pies and paper dolls.

BOTANY

Botany or the study of plants should be taken up by the Scouts both on account of its usefulness and also as a means to cultivate the faculty of observation. It is really wonderful how the observation can seem to grow day by day. I know a small girl who has been collecting specimens of plants only one day a week for one season, but she can now find rare plants and obscure little blossoms. Keep a note of all these and make a collection. It may at some time be very valuable. Find out what plants have medicinal qualities. Some localities are remarkable for a great variety of medicinal plants and frequently the manufacturers of medicines are glad to know where they can be procured. Within a radius of a few miles from Charleston, S. C., there are more medicinal plants than there are in the whole State of New York.

Cultivated plants, too, can be studied with excellent results. Watch the growth of any little house plant and see the effect of different soil and temperature upon it. From the time of planting to flowering and seeding full notes should be made in a book, and this will be quite a treasure in the years to come as your first independent attempt to study botany.

As soon as excursions are made into the fields or woods some regular observations may be made and systematically recorded upon a selected class of plants. It is not best for all to study the same things but different patrols or groups of individuals from the same patrol may devote their attention to a variety of plants, exchanging specimens and notes. Thus a much wider field of study is opened to all. Some may, for instance, take up the study of the oaks and others of the nut-trees. While some are studying vines of the smilax group another set of notes is being made of the grapes.

For this purpose a good reference book dealing with the plants of your locality is necessary.

Trees

Outline, for example, a study of the family of oaks.

In the first place the acorn or seed of the oak is in a cup. This is the distinguishing mark of the family.

No matter what the shape of the leaves or the size of the tree if it bears an acorn it is an oak. Chapman divides the family into those that bear every year and those that bear only every other year. That seems at first to be a serious stumbling-block, but there is a way to get over that, for as to the fruit we only need to study that which we find and leave the others for another year. We do not expect to do it all at once. Our next consideration is the leaves. First those that are entire, then three-lobed; others are long stemmed and deeply lobed. Of these last we will find two subclasses—those smooth on the under surface and the others somewhat fuzzy. Some can be classed as "sinuate lobed" and others as toothed and many other distinctions as they arise serve to mark perfectly well the different species. In the book before me twenty species and ten varieties or subspecies are described.

Our definite study of these groups need not interfere at all with the general collection of the seasons' wild flowers as they come along. From week to week each patrol can have a list posted of the flowers to be expected in the woods and fields. To this can be added with profit the birds due to arrive or to nest. The lists of "possibles" and the results as shown by note-books will of course show great gaps but will be a pleasant incentive to competitive exploring trips. Then, too, the unexpected is sure to happen, and the glory of a discovery adds a charm which must be felt before it can be understood. Above all learn correct names. Latin names are not harder to remember than any other new names and lead to no confusion.

Now let us look back and see what all this Nature study teaches the Scouts in their course of training as Scouts. First and foremost is the habit of careful and close observation—not only how much we can see but how correctly we see it. Second habits of order—we group our knowledge in the best and most scientific manner. We have a regular plan of procedure. And last kindness—general humanity to all living things. We look with new eyes even at the bright-eyed little toad that hops across the path. We do not tear or deface the spider's web. It becomes a new joy to find the first spring flower or some late lingering bloom in the fall. And a new one—one strange to the locality is a triumph to be long talked about. Last night a saw-whet owl sang to me. From a strictly musical standpoint his efforts were far from dulcet, but it is the second record of his appearance in this county so it filled me with gladness as no orchestra could have done. One of my little Girl Scouts found a pipsissewa flower in December. I know she will always be glad, for it is not due to bloom till spring. It was the *Pyrola maculata*.

In talking about these Nature studies I have said nothing about walking. We walk too little in America. Between the trolley car and the automobile the noble art of walking seems in danger of being lost. To use an expressive slang phrase "it's up to" the Scouts to revive and preserve it. What better inducement can be offered for a good long walk than the study—systematic study—of Old Dame Nature's many secrets and unsurpassable beauties.

STARS

How to Find the Time by the Stars

FIG. 1 shows the stars around the northern pole of the heavens (Pole Star), and the Pointers of the Great Bear, which direct us to the Pole Star.

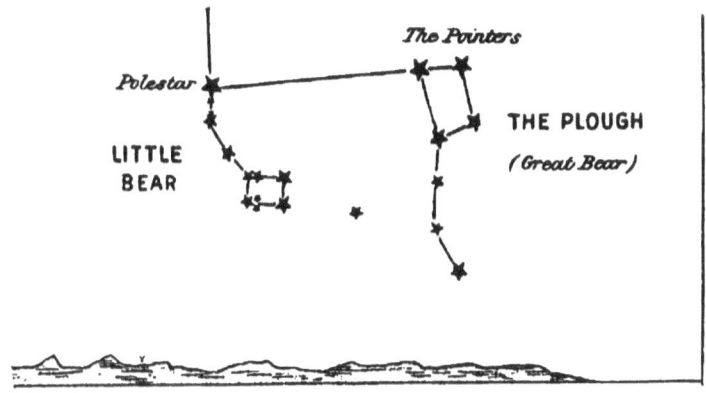

FIG. 1.

Since all stars appear to rise in the East and set in the West (which is really due to our earth turning round under them), the Pointers revolve once around the Pole Star in the opposite direction to the hands of a clock, once in twenty-four hours, or they swing through a quarter of a circle once in six hours; it is thus a simple matter after a little practice to judge what part of the imaginary circle they will pass through in an hour or less.

Assuming that all the stars rise four minutes earlier each night, and that the Pointers of the Plough are vertically above the Pole at midnight at the end of February, we may easily calculate the position of the Pointers for any hour of the night.

56 HOW GIRLS CAN HELP THEIR COUNTRY

The Star Clock

Example. To find the position of the Pointers say on the 15th of April at midnight.

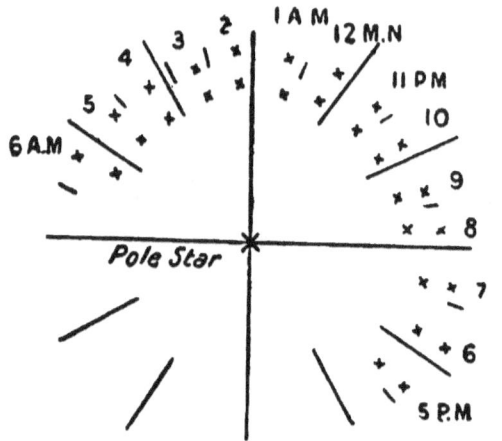

FIG. 2.—NORTHERN HEMISPHERE.

March 31 days + April 15 days = 46 days × 4 minutes = 184 minutes divided by 60 minutes = 3 hours and 4 minutes. Therefore the Pointers will be to the left of the perpendicular pointing down to the right at just over an angle of 45° or half a right angle (3 hours).

Then there is another set of stars representing a man wearing a sword and a belt, named "Orion." It is easily recognized by the three stars in line, which are the belt, and three smaller stars in another line, close by, which are the sword. Then two stars to right and left below the sword are his feet, while two more above the belt are his shoulders, and a group of three small stars between them make his head.

Now the great point about Orion is that by him you

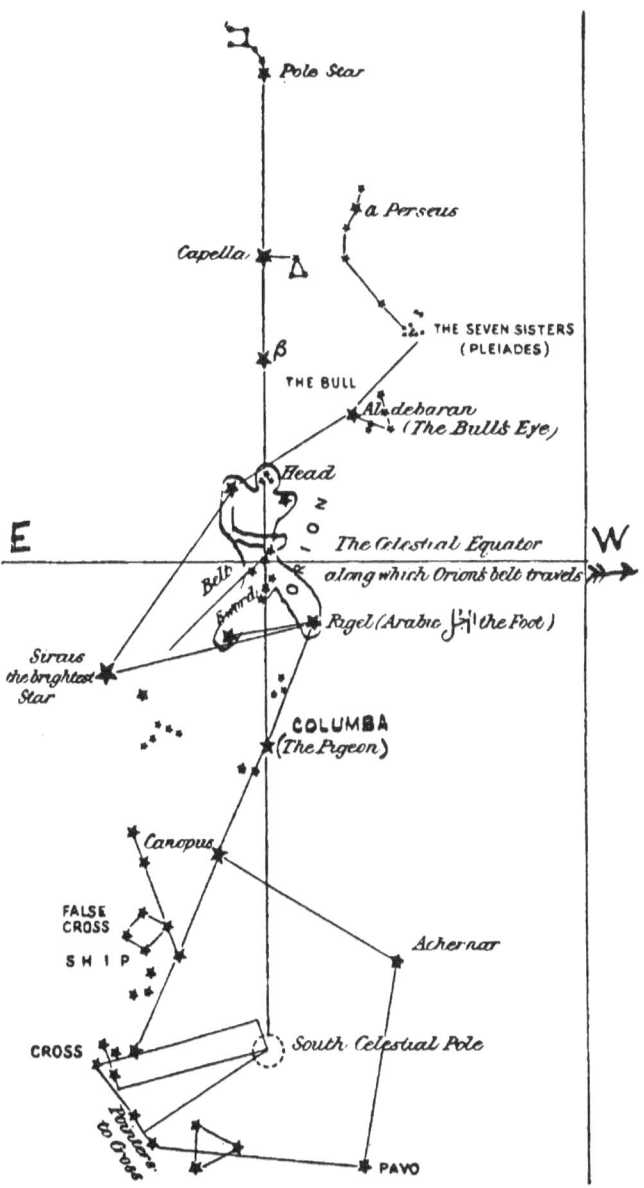

Fig. 3.

can always tell which way the North or Pole Star lies, and which way the South, as you can see him whether you are in the South or the North part of the world. The Great Bear can only be seen when you are in the North, and the Southern Cross when you are in the South.

If you draw a line by holding up your staff against the sky, from the center star of Orion's belt through the center of his head, and carry that line on through two big stars till it comes to a third, that third one is the North or Pole Star.

Then if you draw a line the other way, beginning again with the center star of the belt, and passing through the center star of the sword, your line goes through another group of stars shaped like the letter L. And if you go about as far again past L, you come to the South Pole, which unfortunately is not marked by any star. Roughly Orion's sword, the three small stars, points North and South.

East and West. Orion sets due west, and rises due east, so that, if you can catch him rising or setting, you know where the points of the compass are. Constellations, such as Orion, or the Bull, rise in the east, four minutes earlier each succeeding night—that is about half an hour earlier every Saturday.

The Mariner's Compass

Boxing the compass consists in enumerating the points beginning with north and working around the circle as follows:

North	East, Northeast
North by East	East by North
North, Northeast	East
Northeast by North	East by South
Northeast	East, Southeast
Northeast by East	**Southeast by East**

HELP THEIR COUNTRY

Southeast
Southeast by South
South, Southeast
South by East
South
South by West
South, Southwest
Southwest by South
Southwest
Southwest by West
West, Southwest
West by South
West
West by North
West, Northwest
Northwest by West
Northwest
Northwest by North
North, Northwest
North by West
North

Fig. 4.

Many people know hardly a single star by name. Scouts will do well to take some notice of the stars when in camp and if possible learn names and habits, for these stars have habits—habits that are ruled by very stringent laws. In the Almanac you will find the names of the evening and morning stars for different parts of the year, but strange to say they are not stars but planets or worlds like ours. Sometimes a bright star that is really a star rises before the sun and this must not make any confusion in your studies in "star gazing"; it can readily be distinguished and named by reference to some book or by asking some astronomer. Learn enough certainly to find the North Star or Polaris as it is called by scientific men. It is easily found by following the Pointers of the "Big Dipper"—the Great Bear or Ursa Major, sometimes called the "Plough." Orion is a good winter constellation for you to know and the Scorpion—or Scorpio—is visible in the summer.

Telling the Time by Stars

One of the best star groups from which to estimate the time is the Big Dipper or Great Bear as astronomers call it—Ursa Major. In January this is to the west or right of the North or Pole-star and in June to the east or left. When exactly above or below at these times of year respectively it is midnight. At other times of the year it will be at intermediate positions and must be located and judged accordingly. The two Pointers are about five degrees apart and make a good measure to judge of distances in the sky.

When an almanac is available the time of rising and setting of the moon gives a moderately accurate way to fix at least one time in the night. The relative positions of some of the large stars can be judged from that as a fixed time. However in camp life it is about as easy to say, "The morning star is up and it will soon be daylight" or "The evening star has not set so it can't be bedtime."

When there is a full moon it will always be south at midnight. And if a pale sickly looking little moon comes climbing up in the east it is safe to say, "Morning is not far off." Accuracy farther than this is not possible except with good instruments. At the sea-shore the tides are a better way to judge the time than the stars.

The Sun Clock

When you have been able to find the North Star it will be very easy to set up a sun-dial. This is not so very useful now that standard time is so universally used but still it is fine practice and knowing the difference between "sun time" and standard time can be referred to with a fair amount of accuracy and many people regard it as a curiosity.

Select a place where the sun shines all day and the ground is level. Set up a post or stake perpendicular and firm. At night go and "sight" a straight stick at the North Star and fasten it securely. This stick will now be parallel to the axis of the earth and its shadow will fall at the same spot on any given hour no matter what season of the year it may be. At noon by the sun the shadows of the slanting stick and the upright one will coincide. This gives you the "sun noon" and the time by a standard watch or clock will tell you what correction to apply to your dial to convert its time into standard. Having once established the noon, or "no hour" mark the I, II, III, IV, V, and VI can be marked with stakes. Then calculate the correct sun time of VI A.M. by your standard watch and stake out the morning hours. Halves and even quarters can be marked between if you wish.

A flower dial can be made by having your upright post a pretty tall one, say ten or even twenty feet, and planting rows of flowers like spokes of a wheel along the hour lines. It may be possible even to select such as are likely to open at or near the indicated hour. The entire semicircle of pegs will also make a pretty finish with tall ornamental foliage plants or shrubs.

Hints to Instructors

PRACTICE

Make a sun-dial on the ground, mark the hours with stones or sticks, and see if it shows the time every day.

62 HOW GIRLS CAN HELP THEIR COUNTRY

Send out Scouts in pairs to compete with each other to gain the same spot, but going by different routes (if needed, find their way by map); to reach the church or station or other places without being seen by the others on the way; give marks for the quickest. If possible, the instructor will have left a letter or sweets there overnight for the winners to bring back.

Among the Stars

Scouts must be able to find their way by night, but unless they practise it they are very apt to lose themselves. At night distances seem much greater, and land-marks are hard to see.

When patrolling in dark places, keep closer together, and in the dark or in the woods or caves keep in touch with each other by catching hold of the end of the next Scout's staff.

The staff is also useful for feeling the way.

Winter Evenings.—*Cut out a quantity of little stars from stamp edging. Take an old umbrella, open, and stick the stars inside it, in the patterns of the chief constellations, then hold it overhead, and turn it once round for twenty-four hours, making the stars rise in the east.*

The sun and the moon appear almost the same size as a rule. When we are a little nearer the sun, in winter, he looks a trifle larger than the moon.

To study the constellations, go out when the stars are bright armed with a star map and a bicycle lamp to read it by, and spread a rug on the ground to lie on, or have a deck-chair, or hammock. Look out for shooting meteors in August and November.

Let each girl try to draw a sketch map of a given constellation, from memory.

GARDENING

Now what about the gardens, for it goes without saying that Girl Scouts must have gardens. Getting right down and smelling the fresh soil is good for any one. It is mother earth's own breath. Watching the growth of our seeds is a veritable joy of joys. But what had we better plant. Why not let every one plant at least one tree? Never mind what kind of a tree. We will talk about that in a minute but decide at the outset that you will have at least one tree growing this year. Your trees will be a legacy to posterity from the Girl Scouts to their country. For in this United States of ours we have cut down too many trees and our forests are fast following the buffalo. Nay, the bare face of the land has already begun to prove less attractive to the gentle rains of heaven and offers far too open a path to the raw blasts of winter. In many sections of our country the climate is drier and colder than it was before so much of the forest was destroyed. We are just waking up to the sad fact which it will take many years to rectify. So let us plant trees.

A tree is a tree anyway be it large or small. Some are useful food producers while others are of value for ornament or timber. All are good. There are no bad trees. So if you plant and raise a tree there can be no mistake. Whatever kind you select you will have done well. Fruit and nut trees will of course appeal most strongly to the young, especially those with good healthy appetites. Many very young trees can be made to return some fruit in a comparatively short time by being budded or grafted. Scouts should learn how to bud and graft. It is not hard. Pears, plums, figs, and peaches all do well in the South as do also some apples and grapes. Peach trees though are in the main short-lived. But trees of different kinds can be grown all over the country. Apples and pears are at their best in the North and many kinds are very long lived trees. There are apple trees still bearing known to be a hundred years old. Sugar maple does well where there are long winters, and a wood of them—locally called a "sugar bush"—is a paying piece of property. Most fruit trees are best bought from dealers or obtained from your friends. They do not come "true" as it is called from the seed. A Baldwin apple-seed will not produce a Baldwin apple. But as all the varieties are got by selecting from seedlings we can experiment if we wish. I am already saving my apple-seeds for next year, and it will certainly be grand if we can get a nice new kind of apple and name it the Girl Scout.

Don't imagine now because I say so much about trees that I am not going to make any suggestions about flowers. Any and all kinds of flowers will do in your gardens but do not neglect our own wild ones. Take the goldenrod for instance. The finest I have ever seen is grown in a city garden. Many other of our wild flowers will bear cultivating and some well repay the care necessary to "tame" them. The atamasco lily seems to be perfectly at home in the garden and so does the bloodroot. I have never seen any of the orchises in a garden. Violets of course would be favorites if our native species were not with one exception scentless. As any gardener's book will tell you all about our "tame" flowers it is not necessary to say much about them. So I will only just hint "bulbs" and drop the subject.

Useful Flowers

You may some day have a garden of your own—if you have not already—and then you will be able to grow all your own herbs for cooking and for medicines: such as aconite; rosemary, which is good for the hair; poppies,

HELP THEIR COUNTRY 65

which are useful for sleeplessness, but poisonous to eat, as they contain opium; or hops which promote sleep, either stuffed in a pillow, or as tea. Carnations were formerly steeped in casks of wine to flavor the wine. St-John's-wort was used for headaches and fevers and to cure serpent-bites. Its other name is tout-sain or heal-all; and if you wear it it will keep off all designs of evil spirits. Mallow blossoms are good for throat complaints. Sunflower buds were boiled and eaten with oil and vinegar; and sunflower seeds roasted and ground make a sort of coffee, and uncooked are food for fowls. They are also a cure in whooping-cough. Lime-tree blossom tea is good for colds and promotes perspiration, and bees love lime-blossom for their honey. The bark of the lime is particularly useful for making mats and bast for tying with. It is sometimes called the linden-tree, and that is how Linnæus got his name. His ancestors lived under a great lime-tree. The scent of flowers comes out at night. Dandelion tea is a tonic, and is good for one's liver. Saffron flowers dried are used in cakes, and for coloring lace and stuffs a delicate yellow. If you can find any groundsel it is useful boiled as a poultice to cure wasp stings.

Part III

HOME LIFE

SANITATION

GIRL SCOUTS should do everything in their power to make and keep their homes healthy as well as happy.

Most of you cannot choose your own dwelling, but whether you live in a house, a cottage, a flat, in rooms, or even in one room of a house, you can do a very great deal to keep it healthy and pure.

Fresh air is your great friend; it will help you to fight disease better than anything else. Open all your windows as often as you can, so that the air may get into every nook and corner. Never keep an unused room shut up. You know what a stagnant pool is like—no fresh water runs through it, it is green and slimy, and full of insects and dead things; you would not care to bathe in it. Well, still and stuffy air in a house is very much worse, only, unluckily, its dangers cannot be seen, but they are there lying in ambush for the ignorant person. Disease germs, poisonous gases, mildew, insects, dust, and dirt have it all their own way in stale, used-up air.

You do not like to wash in water other people have used, but it is far worse to breathe air other people have breathed. Air does not flow in and flow out of the same opening at the same time any more than water does, so you want two openings in a room—an open window to let the good air in, and a fireplace and chimney to let the stale air out, or where there is no fireplace, a window open both at top and bottom. The night air in large towns is purer than the day air, and both in town and country you should sleep with your

WASHING.

IRONING.

window open if you want to be healthy. Draughts are not good, as they carry away the heat from your body too fast; so if your bed is too near the window, put up a shelter between it and the open window, and cover yourself more. At least one window on a staircase or landing should always be kept open, and also the larder and the closet windows.

Tidiness

Motto: "TIDY AS YOU GO."

Half your time will be saved if little things are kept tidy. Have a place for everything, and have everything in its place. If you are not sure which is the right place for a thing, think "*Where, if I wanted it, should I go to look for it?*" That place is the right one. Get into the habit of always making a hank of any string you get, and collect them.

War must be waged against rats and mice, or they will invade you and loot everything. If you have no mouse-traps, put a newspaper over a pail of water, break a hole slightly in the center in the form of a star, and place a bit of herring or cheese on the center tips of star to entice the mouse. Let the paper reach to the floor not too upright, for the mouse to climb up. Try putting broken camphor into their holes; they dislike the smell. Fly and wasp traps are made by tying paper over a tumbler half-filled with water and beer or treacle. Break a hole in the paper, and fit in a tube of rolled paper about one inch long and one inch across.

Try to keep yourself neat, and see that the house you live in is clean, sweet, and pleasant.

The Woodpecker

When you find that the ground round a tree is strewn with tiny chips of wood you may know at a glance that a woodpecker is making her nest there. The woodpecker chips away the bark and makes a deep hollow in the trunk. But she has sense enough to know that the chips which fall are tell-tales, so you may see her making efforts to tidy up the place, and in the end she will go to the trouble of flying away with every little chip and scrap in her beak to a distance, so that no enemy can see that she has been cutting a hole in that tree.

DAMP is never healthy, but you can prevent it to a great extent by letting plenty of fresh air go through your house and rooms which have been shut up.

When you see signs of damp, try to find out the cause; it may be put right. A pipe or gutter may have got blocked, or there may be a loose slate, or the water pipes may be leaking.

In countries where there are mosquitoes people are very careful not to allow any water to lie near their houses, for the poisonous mosquito breeds in stagnant water. Sunflowers planted near a house help to keep the soil dry; also low bushes and plants. Consumption and other deadly disease germs flourish in damp, ill-aired houses.

SUNLIGHT is a great health-giver and disinfectant, and the more of it you have in your house the better. Long ago people used to shut out the sun and air for fear their curtains and carpets would fade, but it is far better that the sun should fade your curtains than that the darkness should fade you. Cases of consumption are rare in dry, sunny houses.

Nurseries and bedrooms should have plenty of morning and midday sun.

CLEANLINESS in every part of the house is most necessary, especially kitchens and larders. Do not let dust or rubbish collect anywhere, behind furniture or pictures, under beds, or in cupboards. If we realized what horrid things we may collect from pavement or

HELP THEIR COUNTRY

street dust on our skirts and boots, we should be much more careful about the dusting of our rooms.

Do not allow dogs, cats, or birds to be where they can touch your food or your cooking utensils; animals have diseases too. Flies, gnats, and fleas are most dangerous pests; they feed on decayed and diseased things, and may carry poison on their feet, and leave it on your food. Keep them out of your house, and especially chase them out of your kitchen and larder. Any bad smell in a house is a danger signal; find out its cause, and get rid of it.

Be sure your drinking water is pure. If you are at all doubtful about it *boil it well*—that is, for not less than fifteen minutes. Water cisterns should be often cleaned out. See that all drains, sinks, and closets are in good order. A very poisonous gas called sewer-gas comes from bad drains, and typhoid, diphtheria, etc., are caused by bad drinking water and bad drainage. The gas does not come up if there is a "trap" full of water in the pipe; that is a curve in the pipe where water collects. Let water run down all sinks once or twice a day to rinse the pipes. To sum up, Mrs. Benson says: "Remember that nearly all the *dangers* to health in a house or room begin with a D, and these dangers or destroyers are:

"Darkness,
"Damp,
"Dust,
"Doubtful drinking water,
"Defective drains."

Against these destroyers, which bring debility, disease, and even death, the Scouts' defences are:

"Sunlight,
"Fresh air,
"Cleanliness."

HEALTH

Exercises and their Object

To make yourself strong and healthy it is necessary to begin with your inside, and to get the blood into good order and the heart to work well; that is the secret of the whole thing, and physical exercises should be taken with that intention. This is the way to do it:

(a) *Make the heart strong* in order to pump the blood properly to every part of the body, and so to build up flesh, bone, and muscle. *Exercise:* "Swimming" and "Wrist Pushing."

(b) *Make the lungs strong* in order to provide the blood with fresh air. *Exercise:* "Deep breathing."

(c) *Make the skin perspire* to get rid of the dirt from the blood. *Exercise:* Bath, or rub with a damp towel every day.

(d) *Make the stomach work* to feed the blood. *Exercise:* "Body bending," "Roller and Rocker."

(e) *Make the bowels active* to remove the remains of food and dirt from the body. *Exercise:* "Body-bending" and "Kneading the abdomen." Drink plenty of good water. Punctual daily move of bowels.

(f) *Work muscles in each part of the body* to make the blood circulate to that part, and so increase your strength. *Exercise:* Walking, and special exercises of special muscles.

The blood thrives on simple good food, plenty of exercise, plenty of fresh air, cleanliness of the body both *inside* and out, and proper rest of body and mind at intervals.

The Japs are particularly strong and healthy. They eat very plain food, chiefly rice and fruit, and not much of it. They drink plenty of water, but no spirits. They take lots of exercise. They make themselves good-tempered. They live in fresh air as much as possible

HELP THEIR COUNTRY

day and night. Their particular exercise is Ju-Jitsu, which is more of a game than drill, and is generally played in pairs. By Ju-Jitsu, the muscles and body are developed in a natural way, in the open air as a rule. It requires no apparatus.

The Nose

Always breathe through the nose. Fifty years ago Mr. Catlin wrote a book called *Shut your Mouth and Save your Life*, and he showed how the Red Indians for a long time had adopted that method with their children to the extent of a cruel habit of tying up their jaws at night, to ensure their breathing only through their nose.

Breathing through the nose prevents germs of disease getting from the air into the throat and stomach; it also prevents a growth in the back of the throat called "adenoids," which are apt to stop the breathing power of the nostrils, and also to cause deafness.

For a Scout nose-breathing is also specially useful.

By keeping the mouth shut you prevent yourself from getting thirsty when you are doing hard work. And also at night, if you are in the habit of breathing through the nose, it prevents snoring. Therefore practise keeping your mouth shut and breathing through your nose.

Ears

A Scout must be able to hear well. Generally the ears are very delicate, and once damaged are apt to become incurably deaf. People are too apt to fiddle about with their ears in cleaning them by using things which are dangerous to such a sensitive organ as the ear, the drum of the ear being a very delicate, tightly stretched skin which is easily damaged. Very many children have had the drums of their ears permanently injured by getting a box on the ear.

Eyes

A Scout, of course, must have particularly good eyesight; she must be able to see anything very quickly, and to see it a long way off. By practising your eyes in looking at things at a great distance they will grow stronger. While you are young you should save your eyes as much as possible, or they will not be strong when you get older; therefore avoid reading by lamplight or in the dusk, and also sit with your back or side to the light when doing any work during the day; if you sit facing the light it strains your eyes.

The strain of the eyes is a very common failure with growing girls, although very often they do not know it, and headaches come most frequently from the eyes being strained; frowning on the part of a girl is very generally a sign that her eyes are being strained. Reading in bed brings headaches.

Teeth

Bad teeth are troublesome, and are often the cause of neuralgia, indigestion, abscesses, and sleepless nights. Good teeth depend greatly on how you look after them when you are young. Attention to the first set of teeth keeps the mouth healthy for the second teeth, which begin to come when a child is seven and these are meant to last you to the end of your life, if you keep them in order.

If one tooth is allowed to decay, it will spread decay in all the others, and this arises from scraps of food remaining between the teeth and decaying there.

A thorough Scout always brushes her teeth inside and

outside and between all, just the last thing at night as well as other times, so that no food remains about them to rot. Scouts in camps or in the wilds of the jungle cannot always buy tooth-brushes, but should a tiger or a crocodile have borrowed yours, you can make your teeth just as bright and white as his are by means of a frayed-out dry, clean stick.

Hints to Instructors

MEASUREMENT OF THE GIRL

It is of paramount importance to teach the young citizen to assume responsibility for her own development and health.

Physical drill is all very well as a disciplinary means of development, but it does not give the girl any responsibility in the matter.

It is therefore deemed preferable to tell each girl, according to her age, what ought to be her height, weight, and various measurements (such as chest, waist, arm, leg, etc.). She is then measured, and learns in which points she fails to come up to the standard. She can then be shown which exercises to practise for herself in order to develop those particular points. Encouragement must afterwards be given by periodical measurements, say every three months or so.

Cards can be obtained from the "Girl Scouts" Office, which, besides giving the standard measurements for the various ages, give columns to be filled in periodically, showing the girl's remeasurements and progress in development. If each girl has her card it is a great incentive to her to develop herself at odd times when she has a few minutes to spare.

Teach how to make camp tooth-brushes out of sticks. "Dragonroot" sticks for cleaning teeth can be got at chemists' shops as samples.

My Physical Development

Date.	Weight.	Height.	Chest Expanded.	Neck.	Forearm.	Biceps.

Fill in this page quarterly, the progress shown should be a useful incentive.

Games to Develop Strength

Skipping, rowing, fencing, swimming, tennis, and handball are all valuable aids to developing strength.

High jump, long jump, vaulting, pole jump.

Staff exercises, to music if possible. Maze and spiral; follow-my-leader, done at a jog-trot in the open air. A musical accompaniment when possible. If done indoors,

HELP THEIR COUNTRY

all the windows in the room must be kept open top and bottom. Sing the tune.

FLAGS.—Choose sides; each player lays down a flag or a handkerchief at her own goal, and each side tries to capture the flags of the other; once she touches the opponent's flag she cannot be taken prisoner, but goes back with the flag to her side.

Players can rescue a prisoner by touching her in prison. Players should keep moving as much as possible all the time, and try to evade being captured.

PRACTISE throwing at a mark. Put a pebble on the top of a staff and stand at a certain line so many paces off.

Morris dances (old English country dances) and the folk-songs.

ENDURANCE IS USEFUL

READ.—Have you not often heard of accidents on the ice? In the winter of 1895 some schoolgirls were sliding on a frozen canal, when one girl twelve years old ventured into the middle. Then there was an ominous cracking, and in a moment she was struggling in water many feet deep.

Miss Alice White, a teacher, happened to witness the accident. Notwithstanding the warnings of several persons standing on the towing-path, who assured her it was most dangerous, she at once went on the ice and approached as close to the hole as she dared with safety. She then lay down at full length, so as to more equally distribute her weight, and tried to seize the struggling child. But under her weight the ice broke, and the brave girl was precipitated into the cold water. The bystanders shouted to her to forsake the child, and at least save her own life, but she did nothing of the kind. She held on to her precious burden, and literally fought her way out. Piece after piece of the ice broke off, but she at length reached the bank in a state of great exhaustion. Her hands were cut in many places by the sharp ice, but they were wounds of which any one might well have been proud. Miss White was only sixteen years old, and it was the second time she had saved a life.

Laying a pole or a branch across the hole is a good plan.

An Easy Way to Grow Strong

It is possible for any girl, even though she may be small and weak, to make herself into a strong and healthy woman if she takes the trouble to do a few body exercises every day. They only take about ten minutes, and do not require any kind of apparatus such as dumb-bells, parallel bars, and so on.

This should be practised every morning, the first thing on getting up, and every evening before going to bed. A girl of ten years should weigh at least fifty pounds, the average height at that age being forty-nine inches. The value of this exercise is much increased if you think of the object of each move while you are doing it, and if you are very particular to breathe the air in through your nose. A great many people who are pale and seedy are made so by living in rooms where the windows are seldom opened and the air is full of poisonous gases or germs. Open your windows, especially at the top, every day to let the foul air out.

Do not exercise immediately *after* eating; let your meal rest.

Girls who have not done these exercises before should begin them gradually with care, bit by bit, doing more every day. Brush your hair, clean your teeth, wash out your mouth and nose, drink a cup of cold water, and then go on with the following exercises.

It is best to carry these out with as few clothes on as possible, either in the open air or close to an open window. The movements should all be done as slowly as possible.

Housewifery

Every Girl Scout is as much a "hussif" as she is a girl. She is sure to have to "keep house" some day, and whatever house she finds herself in, it is certain that that place is the better for her being there.

Too many odds and ends and draperies about a room are only dust-traps, and rugs or carpet squares, which can be taken up easily, are better than nailed down carpets. Keep all the furniture clean and bright. Fresh air, soap, and water are the good housewife's best allies. Bars of soap should be cut up in squares, and kept for six weeks before being used. This hardens it, and makes it last longer.

In scrubbing boarded floors, the secret is not to deluge the floor; change the water in the pail frequently.

In the work of cleaning think out your plan beforehand, so as not to dirty what has been cleaned. Plan out certain times for each kind of work, and have your regular days for doing each thing.

PASTE-BOARDS AND DEAL TABLES.—Scrub hard the way of the grain. Hot water makes boards and tables yellow. Rinse in cold water, and dry well.

SAUCEPANS.—New saucepans must not be used till they have first been filled with cold water and a little soda, and boiled for an hour or so, and must be well scoured. After basins or saucepans have been used fill them at once with cold water to the brim; this will prevent anything hardening on the saucepan, and will make cleaning easier.

Needlework

"A stitch in time saves nine." I cannot agree with this favorite saying, because I feel sure it saves so many more than nine, besides saving time and preventing looking untidy.

I will tell you another thing I don't believe in. Tailors, who are such neat workers, will say that they never pin their work first. If you are not a tailor, it is much better to place your work, before you begin, with plenty of pins. You will never get straight lines or smooth corners if you do not plan and place it all first, just as it has got to be, and tack it there.

Have you noticed that thread is very fond of tying itself into a bow; but this can be prevented by threading the cotton into the needle before you cut it off the reel, making your knot at the end you cut.

Rough measures may be said to be one inch across a twenty-five cent piece, and a yard from nose to thumb, as far as you can reach. Needlework is good for all of us; it rests and calms the mind. You can think peacefully over all the worries of Europe whilst you are stitching. Sewing generally solves all the toughest problems, chiefly other peoples'.

Pillow lace needs a little more attention, but is a lovely art which girls can easily master. I was taught to make the flowers of Honiton lace by a little Irish girl, and the variations you can invent are endless. You would find a good sale for insertion lace of the Torchon patterns. Make your own pillow, and buy some cheap bobbins to begin learning with, and do not try fine work at first. Learn to spin wool and thread; a spinster can earn money in this way.

The Girl Scouts' Patch

I don't know whether you ever did such a thing as burn a hole in your dress, but I have, and if it is in the front, oh, dear! what will mother say. Now, there is a very good way that Girl Scouts have of making it all right and serviceable; they put in a piece and darn it in all round. If possible, get a piece of the same stuff, then it will not fade a different tint, and will wear the

HELP THEIR COUNTRY

same as the rest. You may undo the hem and cut out a bit, or perhaps you may have some scraps over from cutting out your dress.

The piece must be cut three or four inches larger than the hole, and frayed out on all four sides. Trim the hole with your scissors neatly all round quite square with the thread. Then lay your piece over the hole— of course on the back or "wrong side"—and tack it there with cotton. Now take a darning needle, and thread each thread in turn, and darn each one into the stuff. If the ends of stuff are very short, it is best to run your needle in and out where you are going to darn, and then, before pulling it through, thread it with the wool. This patching is excellent for table-linen.

I once had an aunt who was a thorough old Scout, and was rather proud of her mending, she always said that she didn't mind what colored cotton you gave her to sew with, because her stitches hardly ever showed, they were so small, and also she put them inside the stuff. If she was putting on a patch to blue stuff, she could do it with red cotton, and you would never have noticed it on the right side; her stitches were all under the edge. Or else she sewed it at the back, on the wrong side, so that it looked perfectly neat.

If you are not able to match the wool for a darn, it is a good plan to use the ravelings of the stuff itself. Sometimes, away in the country, you can't go to a shop and you have nothing like the piece you want to mend. A Scout would turn it inside out and undo a little of the hem, and ravel out the edge. Suppose you were to cut a hole in the front of your blue serge skirt; if you darn it with the ravelings of the turnings of the seam or the hem, that will be exactly the same color and the same thickness as your dress. No wool you could buy would match as well. Or if you want to mend a jersey or knitted gloves, you never could buy such a good match— the same sized wool and the tints.

Damask table-cloths should be darned to match the pattern, following the flowers of the design, and large holes may be mended like the "Scouts' Patch" just described. To sew on buttons properly, leave them loose enough for the iron to push. On washing articles have your threads long enough to make a little stalk to the button, which is wound round before finishing. Your needle should be sloped out to all sides, so as to take up fresh stuff farther out than the holes in the button.

Scouts could make many useful presents in their spare time, such as cretonne covered blotters or frames, mittens, warm felt slippers (for which woolly soles can be bought), pen-wipers, pin-cushions, and needle-books. They could also make articles for their hospitals, such as night-clothing, soft caps, handkerchiefs, pillow-cases, and dusters.

HOME COOKING

There is a legend in Turkey that when a rich man is engaged to marry a lady he can break it off if she is not able to cook him a dish of dates in a different way every day for a whole month. A friend of ours did somewhat the same in trying a new cook; he always tested them with nothing but cutlets for a fortnight. The real test of a good cook is to see how little food she wastes. She uses up all the scraps, and old bits of bread are baked for making puddings and for frying crumbs; she sees that nothing goes bad, and she also buys cleverly. Those who do not understand cookery waste money.

Perfect cleanliness and neatness should be insisted on, or your food will be bad and unwholesome.

Eggs

Is an egg lighter or heavier when cooked? An experienced cook is experienced in eggs. There are "new

HELP THEIR COUNTRY 81

laid" eggs which are fresh and "fresh" eggs which are not; there are "cooking" eggs which are liable to squeak. Eggs are safe in their shells, and think you don't know whether they are fresh or not, or whether they are raw. Any egg can be thrown out of a first-floor window on to the lawn without the shell breaking; it falls like a cat, right end upwards, and this is not a boiled egg, either! You can tell that because it will not spin on the table, so it must have been a raw egg. A cooked egg would spin.

To tell a stale egg, you will see it is more transparent at the *thick* end when held up to the light.

Fresh eggs are more transparent in the *middle*. Very bad eggs will *float* in a pan of water.

Poached Eggs

Break each egg separately into a cup. When your water is boiling fast, drop in an egg sharply. Use a large deep pan, with salt and vinegar in the water. Lift the egg very carefully in a ladle before it is set too hard. Place the eggs all round a soup plate, pour over them a nice sauce made with flour and butter, a little milk, and some grated cheese and salt.

Meat

Examine the meat before you accept it. If you do not know the looks of good meat, you should go to a butcher's shop, and ask the butcher to show you how to know it. Much gristle is a sign of old age. You can easily tell if meat smells disagreeable. Beef should be of a bright red color, and juicy and elastic. The fat should be firm and of a pale straw color. Mutton should feel dryish, and the fat look white. All papers must be taken off at once. The feet of fowls should be soft and

Fish

A most unwholesome food is stale fish. The gills, if fresh, should be bright red. Tinned fish is often poisonous. Fish is a food which you can get more good from, considering the price, than if you bought meat, and the most nourishing fish is one of the cheapest—that is, the herring. Pieces of fish, buttered, can be deliciously steamed or baked if laid between two plates over a saucepan of water.

Oatmeal

Oats, too, are full of value; a pound and a half a day will keep a hard-working man, for oatmeal increases the power of the muscles, and is rich in bone and flesh-forming materials. What you can get out of oats for 10 cents would cost you $1.00 in lean beef. Oats give increased mental vigor and vitality, as they have so much nerve and brain nourishment in them.

Oatmeal should be kept *fresh* in a shut tin.

If you think your brain requires a fillip, eat plenty of haricot beans, but they must be very much cooked, and should be well buttered. Frumenty is good too.

Beef and mutton, when underdone, are more easily digested than when cooked through.

Roasting and grilling of meat is done over so hot a fire outside that the juices are kept in. The meat has to be frequently turned to prevent it burning, but allow plenty of salt to melt into the meat with the dripping, or it will taste just as good as a sole of a boot.

As Mr. Holding said: "The only method I know of for properly making your meat thoroughly indigestible is to hurry a stew."

HELP THEIR COUNTRY

To stew or braise any meat or fowl you must leave it long on the stove and cook it slowly. Then put in flavoring vegetables, bacon, herbs, and a little stock, and by the time you have done a day's work you will find a dish fit for a king. Even tough meat can be made delicious in this way, so long as it never gets near boiling, and is closely covered. This is a case of "Sow hurry, and you reap indigestion."

Vegetables

Of vegetables I should like to say they can scarcely be too much cooked. Wash well in salted water; let leafy ones have a swim to get rid of grasshoppers and caterpillars and sand, then put them into boiling salted water, and take off the lid. Roots may be allowed lids.

Peel and slice your onions under water, or at a tap.

I once watched a grand *chef* cooking potatoes, and he told me that the best of the potato lies next the skin, so he never cuts it, but he peels his potatoes on a fork after boiling. The cunning cook boils a bunch of mint with the potatoes.

Excellent food for workers are parsnips, beet-roots, or onions.

BOILING MEAT.—If you want the meat and not the juice, you should have your pot boiling fast when the meat is put in. But if you want gravy or beef-tea (not meat), put your meat into cold water, and bring it slowly to the boil.

STOCK POT.—Keep a pot going all day, into which you can put any broken-up bones or scraps left over, to make nourishing broth. Clean turnips, carrots, and onions improve it. Before using let it get cold, so as to skim off the fat.

Barley, rice, or tapioca may be added, and for flavoring, add salt, pepper, chopped parsley, celery, a clove, or mace.

Milk

Milk will take the flavor of any strong smell near it. Stale milk added to fresh will turn the whole of it sour. Sour milk need not be wasted. You can use it for baking or cooking, by adding bicarbonate of soda. Sour milk will clean ink or fruit stains, and in washing it bleaches linen. Yellowed linen should soak in it, so should spoons and forks. Sour milk cleanses oil-cloth as well as women's faces and hands. Chickens and turkeys get fat and lay better for being fed on it.

To WEIGH roughly, tie a loop of string to your packet of tea, sugar, etc., and pass it on to your first finger. I find three pounds is as much as I can hold on my nail. If the loop is shifted to the root of the nail, four pounds is all one can hold. If the string is placed on the first joint, I find the parcel weighs seven pounds. Each person will be different, but you can find out your own power of lifting, and then you will know exactly for the future.

Boiling water is useful to dip your sardine into if you want to get his skin off. But do not dip him into the tea-kettle. To cut very new bread easily, you should put the knife into a jug of boiling water. Cooking in water mostly spoils food, except  greens. Water was never meant to cook with. Water does pretty well for washing in, also as a means of steaming a pan; but if you use it for cooking in, it washes out all the flavor. Cook your food in a covered earthenware jar, standing in water in a covered saucepan.

A problem for cooks is to solve: "What articles cost less after they are manufactured than the raw material costs?" Flour is more expensive than the bread made from it. Cream is more expensive per pint than the butter made from it.

HELP THEIR COUNTRY 85

The true artist in omelettes is one who beats her eggs with a knife on a plate till they are so firm that, on turning the plate upside down, the whites keep sticking to it. A beginner told me she used often to let them drop on the floor; but such was her patience and perseverance that she scraped up all the egg onto the plate again, and continued beating. That is not really necessary for a good omelette.

To make a really good rice pudding let the rice soak in the milk for many hours. The slower it is cooked the better.

Condensed milk is a good substitute for cream.

How to make "crusps."—Put aside any very thin slices of bread (or bread and butter) on the mantelpiece, and in two days they will become delicious "crusps," sweeter and more wholesome than fresh bread.

Kumyss

(An invalid can retain Kumyss when she fails to digest every other nourishment.)

One quart of fresh milk, add two tablespoonfuls of sour milk solidified (or Clabber.)

Let it stand in a china jar or pitcher, lightly covered with a napkin, for twelve hours.

It will then be solidified, take some clean vessel, a pitcher is best—pour the nixture from one vessel to another holding them about ¾ of a yard apart, so the air can strike the milk as it goes down. Pour until the mixture is well broken up (six or eight times) and as smooth as cream. Set aside again in the clean pitcher as before, for twelve hours, then repeat the pouring process. After twelve hours more repeat pouring. It is then done.

Care of Children

There is a school where girls are taught "mothering," and they hire a real live baby to practise upon. We hear that the pupils are taught how to tell by the way the baby cries why it is crying—to know the *hungry cry* the *pain cry*, and the *pins cry*. I want to ask whether the pupils stick pins in to hear the cry, and how would they tell supposing the baby did not cry?

Mrs. Benson writes: " There is no way in which a girl can help her country better than by fitting herself to undertake the care of children. She should learn all she can about them, and take every opportunity of helping to look after these small Girl Scouts and Boy Scouts of the future."

An infant cannot tell you its wants, but a Scout with a knowledge of the needs of children, what to feed them on, and the rules for good health, may save many a baby, for she never knows how soon the precious gift of some child's life may be placed in her hands.

Baby does not know that fire will burn, or that water will drown one, so you need to guard him. Baby requires the proper food to build up a healthy body. He prefers milk for the first months of his life, and even up till three years old he takes mostly milk; and as a baby cannot digest flour, bread, corn-flour, and such things are so much poison to him, they may injure a little baby's health for life. As has been said to older children, let him keep quiet after eating. Even up till three years old, Baby's food must be chiefly milk—biscuits, puddings, and fruit being gradually added. He is very particular about his milk being fresh and good. Baby is extremely punctual. He feels it keenly if you do not feed him at the fixed hour, and will very likely let you know it, and woe betide you if he finds out that you have not properly scalded out his bottle before and after each meal.

When his digestion is not right, his appetite will not be so good. Digestion means that the food you eat is turned into muscle and brain and bone.

We eat onions to make bone, and oats to make brain, but Baby must not be allowed such food till he is older. What is *indigestion?* It means not only uncomfortable pains in the middle of the night, but also that you have not used up the food you ate, and that food is going bad inside you, and making bad blood. Eat only the foods that you know you can digest comfortably. Do not give Baby too much at a time, or he will not be able to digest it, and keep him to plain food.

Air

Sun and Air are life-giving. Put a pale withering plant or human being into the sun, and each will recover health. Give a baby plenty of fresh air, out of doors if you can, but avoid draughty places. Air the rooms well. You know, too, that the air inside the bed-clothes is poison, so do not let Baby sleep with his head under the sheet; tuck it in under his chin. You remember what air did in curing illness in the case of the expressman's children. He had two boys and three little girls all beginning to have consumption, and constantly requiring a doctor at great expense. He got the happy idea of putting them all into his cart when he started out very early on his work, and he drove them about every morning till school time. Every one of them soon got well, and became strong and healthy.

Bath

But no one can be healthy unless they are extremely

clean. Baby will want his bath daily, with soap and warmish water. He likes to kick the water and splash, as long as you support his head. Before starting on this swimming expedition, you should have all his clothes, warm, by you, and all that you will want must be within reach, and he expects a warm flannel on your knees to lie on. You must carefully dry all the creases in his fat body for him, with a soft towel.

Illnesses

What will you do when you suddenly find that Baby is ill. Call in the doctor? Yes—that is, if there is one. But when there is no doctor! You will at once think of all the First Aid you have learnt, and what you know of nursing.

Drugs are bad things. You may ruin a child by giving it soothing drugs and advertised medicines. They sometimes produce constipation. Never neglect the bowels if they become stopped, or you may bring on inflammation. Children's illnesses often are brought on by damp floors; you can trace them to the evening that the boards were washed. A flood of water could not dry without damping the room and the children.

Bowed legs come from walking too soon. It does Baby good to lie down and kick about, for crawling and climbing exercise his muscles.

The best remedy, if you find a child suffering from convulsions, is to place it in a warm bath, as hot as your bare elbow can endure.

Childhood is the time to form the body; it cannot be altered when you are grown up.

Clothing

Children's clothes should be warm but light, and the feet and legs should be kept warm and dry. To put on their stockings, turn the toe in a little way, and poke the toes into the end, then pull over a little at a time, instead of putting the foot in at the knee of the stocking. Put the left stocking on the right foot next day, so as to change them every day.

Flannelette is made of cotton, so it is not warm like wool, and it catches fire easily, as cotton-wool does. Near Dorking some children were acting a Christmas play, and were dressed as angels. One child's veil caught fire in a candle flame, and set light to some cotton-wool on her dress. She rushed to her sisters; but, worse still, she set them on fire, as they were dressed in cotton-wool too. All three were in a terrible blaze, and their mother did her best, getting her own hands burnt in trying to put out the flames. Others came and threw rugs and blankets round the girls, and put out the fire, but still the children were so dreadfully injured that one of them died.

Rubber is most unhealthy, and causes paralysis. Don't sit on rubber or on oilcloth unless covered, and never put rubber next to the skin.

Part IV

HOSPITAL WORK

The training of the Girl Scouts eminently fits them for hospital work. As in the matter of accidents, the statement is made above that the scope of this book is insufficient for a course of instruction, so it is best for the leaders to have lectures, lessons, and demonstrations rather than try to do so little as to condense a delicate subject of this nature into a few paragraphs and so make the reader learn mere rudiments. There is danger in a "little knowledge" of such an important subject. So I will only say that the one important Scout precept of obeying orders is in a hospital of paramount importance. Disobedience is certainly a *crime*.

Nosebleed

Slight nosebleed does not require treatment, no harm results from it. When severe nosebleed occurs loosen the collar (do not blow the nose) apply cold to the back of the neck by means of a key or a cloth wrung out in cold water; a roll of paper under the upper lip between it and the gum will help; when bleeding still continues shove a cotton or a gauze plug into the nostrils leaving it there until the bleeding stops.

Eyes

Dust, flies, or cinder in the eye. Get the person's head well backwards, seize the upper eyelash and pull the upper lid well forward over the lower, press it against the latter as it slips back into place, and if the fly is beneath the upper lid it will be left on the lower lid. If this fails, place a match on the upper eyelid, seize the eyelashes and turn the lid over the match, and if you can see the cause of the trouble remove it with the corner of a handkerchief or use a camel's-hair brush. A drop of castor-oil in the eye soothes it afterwards. For lime in the eye use a weak solution of vinegar and water.

First Aid to Injured

Fire constitutes a danger, especially if there is a panic where the fire starts. Never throw away a lighted match, it may fall on inflammable material and start fire. Reading in bed is dangerous, as if you go to sleep the bed-clothes may catch fire. If you must dry your clothes by a fire watch them carefully.

Cut away all dry grass around a fire in camp.

Never go into a room that smells strongly of escaped gas with a light; never handle gunpowder with matches in your pocket.

How to Put out Fire

If your clothing catches fire don't run for help, that will fan the flames; lie down, roll up in an overcoat or rug. If nothing can be found to roll about you, roll over slowly beating out the flames with your hands. If another person is on fire throw him on the ground and smother the fire with a rug.

What to Do in Case of Fire

Show coolness and presence of mind, throw water (a few bucketfuls will often put out the fire), or blankets, woolen clothing, sand, ashes, dirt, or even flour thrown on it will smother it.

If you discover a fire sound the alarm on the street fire-alarm post, or telephone to the Fire Department. The doors of a house or a room that is on fire should be closed to prevent draughts spreading the flames.

While searching a burning house tie a wet handkerchief over the nose and mouth. The water on the handkerchief gives you a little air. Remember that within six inches of the floor there is no smoke; when you have difficulty in breathing, crawl along the floor with the head low, dragging any one you have rescued behind you. Tie the insensible person's hands together and put them over your head. You can then crawl along the floor dragging the rescued person with you.

Never jump from the window unless the flames are so close that it is your only means of escape. If outside a burning building put mattresses and bedding piled high to break the jumper's fall and get a strong rug to hold, to catch the jumper, and let many people hold the rug. If country districts organize a bucket brigade, two lines of girls from water to fire, pass buckets, jugs, tumblers, or anything that will hold water from girl to girl and throw water on the fire passing buckets back by other line of girls.

Rescue from Drowning

There are four practical methods of bringing a drowning person to land.

1. If quiet, turn him on his back, and grip him by the head so that the palms of the hands cover the ears, and swim on the back. Keep his face above water (Fig. 1).

Fig. 1

STRETCHER DRILL.

Fig. 2

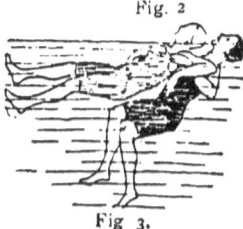

Fig 3.

Fig. 4

2. In case of struggling, turn him on his back. Then grip his arms just above the elbows and raise them until they are at right angles to his body, and swim on the back (Fig. 2).

3. If the arms are difficult to grasp, push your arms under those of the subject, bend them upwards, and place your hands, with the fingers separated, flat on his chest, the thumbs resting on his shoulder joints. Swim on the back (Fig. 3).

4. In rescuing a swimmer with cramp or exhausted, or a drowning person who is obedient and remains quiet, the person assisted must place his hands on the rescuer's shoulders close to the neck at arm's length, turn on his back, and lie perfectly still with the head well back. Here the rescuer is uppermost; and, having his arms and legs free, swims with the breast stroke. This is the easiest method, and enables the rescuer to carry the person a longer distance without much exertion (Fig. 4).

Release

A drowning person will sometimes grip his would-be rescuer in such a manner as to render it impossible to tow him to land. The three following methods are recommended for releasing oneself when clutched by a drowning person.

1. When the rescuer is grasped by the wrists: Extend the arms straightforward, bring them down until they are in a line with the hips, and then jerk the wrists against the thumbs of the subject. This will break the hold (Figs. 5 and 6).

Fig. 5   Fig. 6

2. When the rescuer is clasped round the neck: Take a deep breath and lean well over the drowning person. At the same time, place the left hand in the small of his back. Then pinch the nostrils close between the fingers of the right, while resting the palm on his chin, and push away with all possible force (Fig. 7).

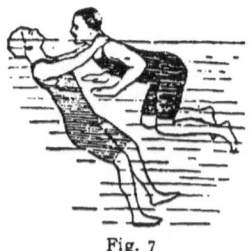

Fig. 7

3. When the rescuer is clasped round the body: Take a deep breath and lean well over as before. Place the left hand on the subject's right shoulder and the right palm on his chin. At the same time bring the right knee against the lower part of his chest. Then by means of a strong and sudden push, stretch your arms and leap straight out, throwing the whole weight of your body backwards (Fig. 8).

Fig. 8

Artificial Respiration

When a person is brought to land in an apparently drowned condition lose no time in attempting restoration. Delay may prove fatal. Act at once and work with caution, continuous energy, and perserverance. Life has, in many cases, been restored after long hours of unceasing work. In all cases send for a doctor as soon as possible. Meanwhile proceed at once to clear the water out of the patient's lungs. The following method is the simplest and is called the Schäfer system, after the inventor. Incline the patient face downwards and the head downwards, so that the water may run out of his mouth, and pull his tongue forward. After running the water out of the patient, place him on his side with his body slightly hanging down, and keep the tongue hanging out. If he is breathing let him rest; if he is not breathing, you must at once endeavor to restore breathing artificially. Here are Professor Schäfer's own instructions:

Fig. 9

1. Lay the patient face downwards with arms extended and the face turned to the side.
2. Don't put a cushion or any support under the chest. Kneel or squat alongside or astride of the patient facing towards his head.

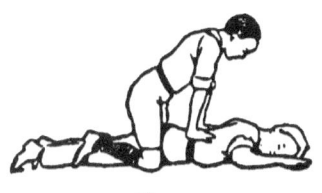
Fig. 10

3. Place your hands on the small of the patient's back, one on each side, with thumbs parallel and nearly touching.
4. Bend forward with the arms straight, so as to allow the weight of your body to fall on your wrists, and then make a firm, steady downward pressure on the loins

of the patient, while you count slowly, "one—two—three."

5. Then swing your body backward so as to relieve the pressure and without removing your hands, while you count slowly, "one—two."

Continue this backward and forward movement, alternately relieving and pressing the patient's stomach against the ground in order to drive the air out of his chest and mouth, and allowing it to suck itself in again, until gradually the patient begins to do it for himself. The proper pace for the movement should be about twelve pressures to the minute. As soon as the patient is breathing you can leave off the pressure; but watch him, and if he fails you must start again till he can breathe for himself.

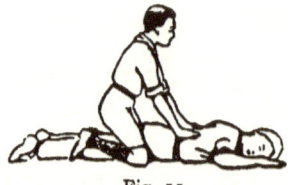

Fig. 11

Then let him lie in a natural position and set to work to get him warm by putting hot flannels or bottles of hot water between his thighs, and under the arms and against the soles of his feet. Wet clothing should be taken off and hot blankets rolled round him. The patient should be disturbed as little as possible and encouraged to sleep while carefully watched for at least an hour afterwards.

Runaway Horses

Don't try to check a runaway horse by standing in front and waving your arms. The horse only dodges you and runs faster. Try to run alongside the vehicle with your hand on the shaft to prevent yourself from falling, seize the reins with the other hand, and drag the horse's head towards you. If you can slow him down by this method you can turn him toward a wall or a house, and he will probably stop.

Ice Rescue

To rescue a person who has broken through the ice, you should first tie a rope around your own body and have the other end tied or held in shore, then get a long board or a ladder, or the limb of a tree, crawl out on this and push it out so that the person in the water may reach it. If nothing can be found on which to support your weight don't attempt to walk to the person to be rescued, but lie flat on your face and crawl out to him, thus so much less weight bears on the ice at one point than walking. Remember if you break through the ice yourself if you try to crawl on the broken ice it will break again with you, better support yourself on edge of ice and await rescue.

Gas and Sewer Gas

Never have the gas faintly burning, partly turned down low, and go to sleep in the room. As gas may escape into the room very big fires in stoves burning in sleeping rooms are dangerous, especially charcoal stoves. In underground sewers and wells dangerous gases are found; if a lighted candle will not burn in such a place it is certain the air will be dangerous for any one entering it.

In rescuing a person in a place filled with gas, take a few deep breaths before entering, carry him quickly out without breathing yourself. Gas will not be found near the floor of a building, so you may be able to crawl out where it would be dangerous to walk.

Treatment and Bandaging the Injured

A fracture is the same thing as a broken bone. When the bone pierces through the skin it is called a compound fracture. When it does *not*, a simple fracture.

If you have to deal with a broken leg or arm, and can't get a doctor at once, make the patient lie down, place the broken leg in same position as sound one, pile around it clothing to keep it in place.

Place the leg in the same position as sound one, and hold it in splints made of anything that is stiff and rigid like a *flat* board (that is better than a round pole) or a limb broken from a tree; shingles make excellent splints.

In applying splints, they should extend beyond the next joint above and the next joint below the broken point. Otherwise the movement of the joint will cause the broken part to move.

With a broken thigh, the splint should be very long, extending from armpit to below the feet, a short splint just below the knee will do for the inner splint.

Splints may be tied on with handkerchiefs, tie firmly, but not so tight as to cause severe pain.

In a fractured thigh it is well to bind the broken leg to the sound one by two or three pieces of cloth around both.

The clothing around the leg makes a padding for the splints unless it is thin summer clothing, in which case straw and leaves should be put between the splint and the leg, or arm.

Fractures of the leg and arm are treated the same way, with splints on inner and outer sides of broken bone.

A sling will be required with fractures of the arm; this may be made with triangular bandage or triangular neck handkerchief or piece torn from your skirt or petticoat. Red Cross outfits are very convenient for injuries.

Compound Fracture

If the sharp edges of the broken bone pierce through the skin, which often happens if splints are not well applied and the person moves, the broken bone then pierces the skin. If a wound is made by the broken bone, then the wound must be treated first. All wounds, unless protected from germs, are liable to become infected

FIRST AID TO THE INJURED.

HELP THEIR COUNTRY

by matter or pus. Blood-poisoning or even death may result. To prevent infection of wounds, a sterilized dressing should be applied; this is a surgical dressing which has been treated so that it is free from germs and can be got at any druggist or can be had in First Aid outfits. Don't handle a wound with your hands or do anything else to it, because even though your hands appear perfectly clean, they are not so, neither is water free from germs, so a wound should never be washed.

If you have no surgical dressing boil a folded towel fifteen minutes; don't touch the inner surface. Apply inner surface of the towel or a clean unused handkerchief to the wound.

How to Stop Bleeding

Keep a person quiet after severe bleeding from a wound as the bleeding may recommence, and give no stimulants unless patient is very weak.

There are two kinds of blood—that which flows from arteries and the blood which flows from veins; the latter is of a dark color and flows in a steady stream and goes back to the heart. A pad firmly tied on such a wound can usually stop the bleeding.

Don't be afraid of leaving a wound exposed to air as it has no germs. When wounds bleed use Red Cross outfit as described on slip contained in outfit.

If an artery is cut a person may bleed to death in a few minutes, so girls should know that the blood from a cut artery is bright red and flows in spirts and jets.

The chief arteries are in the throat. The artery in the upper arm is about in a line with the inner seam of the sleeve of your coat.

The artery in the leg runs down from the center line from the point of the hip in the middle of the crotch in a line with the inseam of trousers.

Pressure should be applied by putting your fingers three inches above the crotch and holding it pressed against the bone. You can feel the artery beating under your fingers, but don't put your finger in the wound as it may infect the latter. While you hold the artery some one else should make a tourniquet, which is a handkerchief tied loosely around the limb and a cork or a smooth stone, placed just above your fingers on the artery. When this is placed, put a stick about a foot long under the handkerchief at the outer side of the limb and twist the stick so that the handkerchief gets tight enough to keep the stone or cork pressing on the artery just as your fingers did at first. Tie the stick in position so it will not slip.

Warning when Using a Tourniquet

Remember that cutting off the circulation for too long is dangerous; don't leave the tourniquet more than an hour. Loosen it and be ready to tighten it quickly if the bleeding recommences.

Another method to stay bleeding from an artery when the injury is below the knee or elbow is to place a pad in the bend and tie the arm or leg bent with the pad tight in the angle of the joint.

If an artery is cut at the throat, jam your fingers into the wound to stop the bleeding or the person may die instantly from loss of blood.

The best stimulant in cases where the patient is very weak is aromatic spirits of ammonia. One teaspoonful in a half-glass of water.

Ivy Poisoning

Avoid poison oak or ivy. If poisoned use carbolized vaseline or baking-soda and water made into a thick paste.

HOW TO CARRY THE INJURED.

To Ease Itching of Midge-bites

For midge and sand-fly bites use listerine and Eucalyptus. Equal quantities or preparation sold by druggist.

Frost-Bite

To prevent frost-bite rub the body when exposed to cold with too little clothing on, because rubbing brings blood to the surface. When the part that was cold suddenly has no feeling, then to restore warmth rub it first with snow or cold water, then gradually with warm water, if hot water is applied at first it may cause mortification in the frozen part.

Part V

PATRIOTISM

History of the Flag

The design for the American flag, Stars and Stripes, was taken originally from General George Washington's family coat-of-arms (which one can still see on the gateposts of the home of his ancestors in England). The flag with its five-pointed stars was first made by a woman. Among the pioneer mothers of America was Betsy Ross. She married John Ross who was killed defending a Colonial storehouse against the British. Betsy's father was a Tory, and as she was herself an ardent patriot she did not return, on her widowhood, to her father's house but conducted the business which her husband had left—that of an upholsterer, and ship furnisher. Betsy's father-in-law was one of the signers of the Declaration of Independence and to his recommendations Betsy owed the distinction of being the maker of the flag, which on June 14, 1777, was adopted as the national colors. Contrary to her advice each new State at first received a stripe as well as a star, until the number of 19 was reached, when they returned to their original design of thirteen stars and stripes, because the States became so numerous that the cycle of stars which formed the original flag had to be changed. The five-pointed star was her suggestion, and it is said that she showed General Washington how to make it from a folded paper. In drawing the star one can do so without lifting the pencil from the paper. This five-pointed star is the Seal of King Solomon and is the sign of infinity. In the desert Mussulmen fanatics draw this sign on the desert sands as a mark of defiance to the infidel.

When the flag is flown at half-mast it is a mark of respect which announces the death of some noted person. When it is flown upside down it is the signal of distress.

America

The first home of social and religious freedom in America was in the Colony of Maryland. When all the other colonies were persecuting every one that did not believe in their own peculiar religious doctrine and making the most invidious social distinctions, Maryland—the Ever Faithful—was a haven of refuge for all. Situated in a middle place among the colonies, her doctrines gradually spread till to-day the proud boast of America is that she is the home of the free. Had the sentiments of Massachusetts prevailed we would have had to-day a most bigoted form of religious government. Had John Locke's Carolina laws lasted we would have been under a grinding oligarchy. Georgia under Oglethorpe's wise management joined hands with Calvert in Maryland, and the result of their joint efforts for the betterment of mankind is the grand Republic of the United States of to-day. Adams and Washington, Franklin and Lincoln are names which shine out from the pages of history to-day and back of each was a good and honored mother. These were patriots—not politicians or place hunters. Throughout our history the emergency seems always to have found the man. And they have been prepared by our great women. For even if a man has not a wife it is seldom that any great thing is done that is not helpe d on by a woman. Girls know your places. They are no mean positions that you are destined to hold. The pages of the history of the future may hold your names in a high and honored place. Do well your part to-day. The work of to-day is the history of to-morrow, and we are its makers. So let us strive to show just as grand names on the pages yet unwritten as are inscribed on those that we have for our proud inheritance.

It is not necessary that every Scout should be proficient in all things suggested for practice. All should be able to drill and know the signs—secret and open—for the use of the organization. They should practise the precepts laid down for their guidance and be above all things "the little friend to all" that makes such a distinctive feature in the work and training of every day's meeting of Scouts. Consider it a paramount duty to attend all meetings and get the most out of the opportunities offered you in the American Band of Girl Scouts. Make your duties amusements and your amusements duties. So will you find that you daily increase in usefulness and your pleasure in life will grow broader. In union there is strength. The Union of Scouts is to be a strong union for the good of our nation in the future and an ever-increasing bond for success to ourselves and aid to others.

The Star-Spangled Banner

O say, can you see, by the dawn's early light,
    What so proudly we hail'd at the twilight's last gleaming?
Whose broad stripes and bright stars, thro' the perilous fight,
    O'er the ramparts we watched were so gallantly streaming;
And the rocket's red glare, the bombs bursting in air,
Gave proof thro' the night that our flag was still there!
O say, does that star-spangled banner yet wave
O'er the land of the free and the home of the brave?

On the shore, dimly seen thro' the mists of the deep,
    Where the foe's haughty host in dread silence reposes.
What is that which the breeze, o'er the towering steep,
    As it fitfully blows, half conceals, half discloses?
Now it catches the gleam of the morning's first beam,
In full glory reflected, now shines on the stream—
'T is the star-spangled banner. O long may it wave
O'er the land of the free and the home of the brave.

And where is that band who so **vauntingly swore,**
   'Mid the havoc of war and the battle's confusion,
A home and a country they'd leave us no more?
   Their blood has washed out their foul footsteps' pollution.
No refuge could save the hireling and slave
From the terror of flight, or the gloom of the grave—
And the star-spangled banner in triumph shall wave,
O'er the land of the free and the home of the brave.

O thus be it ever when freemen shall stand
   Between their loved homes and foul war's desolation,
Blest with vict'ry and peace, may the heav'n-rescued land
   Praise the Power that hath made and preserved us a nation
Then conquer we must, when our cause it is just,
And this be our motto, "In God is our trust"—
And the star-spangled banner in triumph shall wave,
While the land of the free is the home of the brave.

FRANCIS SCOTT KEY.

America

    My country, 't is of thee,
    Sweet land of liberty,
      Of thee I sing;
    Land where my fathers died,
    Land of the Pilgrims' pride,
    From every mountain side
      Let freedom ring.

    My native country, thee,
    Land of the noble free,
      Thy name I love;
    I love thy rocks and rills,
    Thy woods and templed hills;
    My heart with rapture thrills
      Like that above.

    Let music swell the breeze,
    And ring from all the trees
      Sweet freedom's song;
    Let mortal tongues awake,
    Let all that breathe partake,
    Let rocks their silence break,
      The sound prolong!

> Our father's God, to Thee,
> Author of liberty,
>   To thee we sing:
> Long may our land be bright
> With freedom's holy light;
> Protect us by Thy might,
>   Great God, our King.
>
> SAMUEL F. SMITH, 1832.

SELF-DISCIPLINE

Helping Others

ALL Girl Scouts remember that by their promise they are bound to do a good turn to somebody every day. When you get up in the morning you tie a knot in your necktie or handkerchief, which is only untied when you have done something for somebody, even to make room on a seat for some one, to give a thirsty one a drink, whether it be an animal or only a human being, or even to lessen the mind worry of a fellow-creature.

It only counts if you do not take any reward for it or mention it. We can all help by being considerate. Don't shout near hospitals or churches, and stop any noise where there is illness, be quiet where children are being got to sleep, be careful not to start nervous horses. Show that you are thinking of others, so that it will be a good example for passers-by.

Bad Habits

"'T is to-day we make to-morrow."

It is sometimes said that it is as easy to form good habits as it is to form bad ones. But this is not the case, and what we do now becomes a habit to-morrow. It is very easy to get into bad habits and very difficult to get out of them; it often wants a lot of pluck and

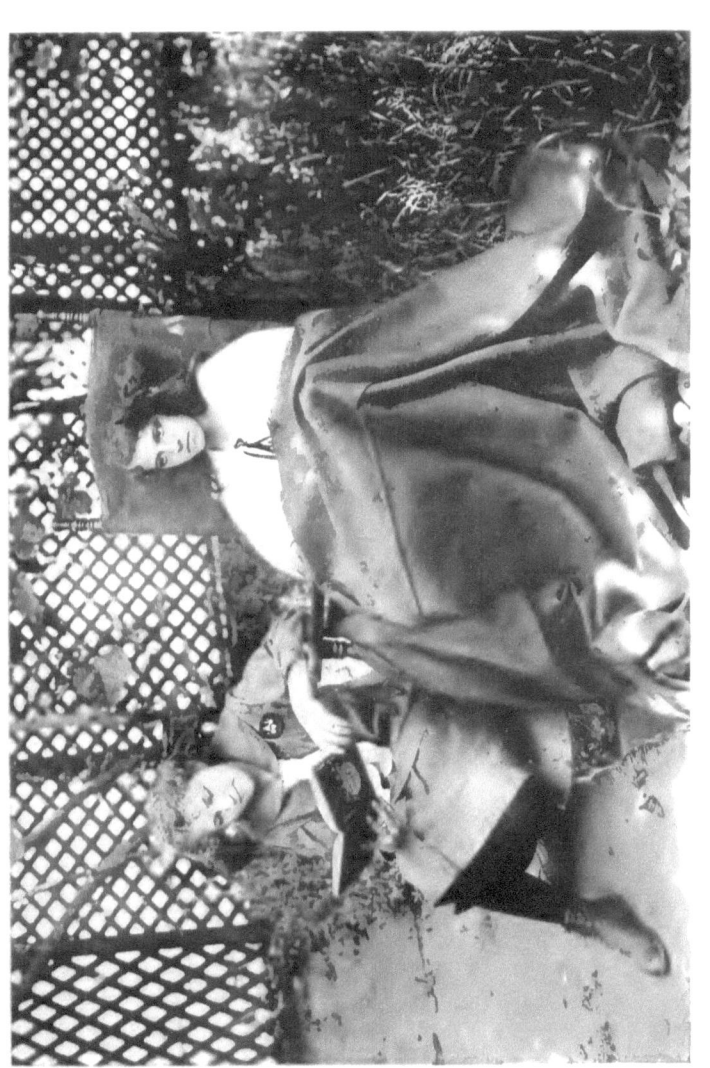

DOING A GOOD TURN.

HELP THEIR COUNTRY

perseverance to get into good habits or to drop bad ones, but you will find that to try is well worth while.

Some girls think it a fine thing to smoke, and start it without thinking; but it is only a silly habit, and by the time they have found out this they find it hard to drop. Other foolish girls get into the way of taking wine or alcohol when they are not well. Instead of doing them good it only does lasting harm, and it is this evil practice which leads to so many women becoming drunkards and ruining their happiness and their homes.

If you are suffering, and girls tell you wine or spirits will make you feel better, refuse it; you know better than they do.

"When in Doubt, Don't"

This motto of grannie's means that when you are not quite sure if it is right to do a thing, then better wait a bit.

Keep clear of girls who tell you nasty stories or talk to you of indecent things. If they see you don't want to join in such bad talk they will soon leave you alone; and each time you refuse to join in nasty talk even the bad girls will in their hearts respect you, and perhaps leave it off themselves, so you will do them good too. And don't read trashy books; keep your mind pure and you will keep happy and healthy.

All secret bad habits are evil and dangerous, lead to hysteria and lunatic asylums, and serious illness is the result; so if you have any sense and courage in you throw off such temptation at once. Resisting temptation will make you more noble. Evil practices dare not face an honest person; they lead you on to blindness, paralysis, and loss of memory.

Your captains and your mother will help you, so if you feel you are not right, just go and talk it over with them. Keep your thoughts as clear as a crystal stream. Thinking evil thoughts blackens the soul.

Humility

Humility, or being humble, was one of the things which was practised by the knights; that is to say, that, although they were generally superior to other people in fighting or campaigning, they never allowed themselves to swagger about it. So don't swagger.

And don't imagine that you have got rights in this world except those that you earn for yourself. You've got the right to be believed if you earn it by always telling the truth, and you've got the right to go to prison if you earn it by thieving; but there are lots of men who go howling about their rights who have never done anything to earn any rights. Do your duty first, and then you will earn your rights afterwards.

Self-Improvement

RELIGION—THRIFT—HOW TO GET ON

Little by Little

"Beautiful days make beautiful years, and beautiful years make a beautiful life."—MILLER.

Modesty

Our Girl Scouts have often been remarked on for their modest bearing. One does not hear them talk about what they have done, or what they are going to do. They just *do* the thing, and say nothing much about it. And, as Miss Rogers writes: "Scouts are modest in their behavior. They go about their business or pleasure quietly and gently, and never draw attention to themselves unnecessarily by behaving noisily and talking or laughing loudly in public. They should be particularly careful of this when in the company of boys or men.

"Girls and boys should be comrades, so never do

HELP THEIR COUNTRY

anything in word or deed to make a boy or a man think less of you, and so lose his respect by making yourself cheap. Remember familiarity breeds contempt. Don't romp about with a boy whom you would n't like your mother or father to see you with.

"Don't let any man make love to you unless he wants to marry you, and you are willing to do so. Don't marry a man unless he is in a position to support you and a family." Moral courage is one thing that all Scouts keep a stock of. Don't be afraid to say you *won't* play at nasty, rude things. When mean girls want you to join in some low fun, when you think it is not right, ask yourself if mother would like to see you doing it; be brave, and have courage to say it is n't right. You will feel twice as happy afterwards.

Every time you show your courage it grows; it becomes easier to be brave after every time you have tried to be courageous.

Reading

Wherever you go you will have the choice of good reading or bad reading, and since what you read has such a lasting effect on your mind, try to read the good and skip the bad. You will not find that trashy novels do you any good. "The reading of novels unfits one's mind for doing good to others."

If you find that you are tempted by reading rubbish, it is easy to stop doing so. Once you *know* what your fault is, you can fight it squarely.

"All your faults are gaining on you every hour that you do not fight them."—RUSKIN.

The thing is, when there is danger before you, don't stop and think about it—the more you look at it the less you will like it—but take the plunge, go boldly in at it, and it won't be half so bad as it looked, when you are once in it. In *Scouting for Boys* it is said this is the way to deal with any difficulty in life. If you get a job or a trouble that seems to you to be too big for you, don't shirk it; smile, think out a way by which you might get successfully through with it, and then go at it, bit by bit, and it will succeed. You can read in *Æsop's Fables* how the old man advised his son that it was easy to break a bundle of rods, but only if you took them one at a time.

Waste

It is supposed that in the "good old times" nobody wasted anything, those good times "when springtime was merry and ale nut-brown, and folk adorned their ordinary conversation with strange imprecations." But nowadays we see a great deal of waste—that is, letting things go that can never be got back. Women and girls have it infinitely more in their power than men have to prevent waste.

The housekeeper and the cook can greatly prevent waste of food, partly by seeing that none goes bad, either meat, vegetables, or bottled groceries; also waste of firing, or lights left on; they can prevent ruining things in washing and cleaning by covering them, also spoiling clothes by wearing aprons; they can oil boots, and mend in good time.

The really orderly Scout has a place for bits. She keeps, for instance, a box for scraps from dressmaking, a drawer for paper and string, a place for collecting what might be given away. In this way she knows where to turn in a moment for anything that is wanted. "A place for everything and everything in its place," which in the end saves time.

Waste of time is the worst of waste. We can never get those moments back again, and it is very nearly impossible to buy time, however much money you have. Now, if you start at once to prevent waste, and plan out where to put the bits you collect, you will be surprised at the amount you get.

Thrift

It sounds easy to learn how to spend money, but it is an art to learn how *best* to spend.

Scouts gain experience by being allowed to purchase for the company, also by keeping the accounts, and they should always keep their own accounts neatly.

We all have to keep accounts when we grow up, and some people have to be careful how much they spend; but in any case, it is as well to get into the way of measuring your expenditure from the first. You will remember that one of the rules in the law of the Scouts is to be thrifty.

Out of those who now read these words, some of you are certain to become rich, and some of you may die in poverty and misery. And it just depends on your own selves which you are going to do.

And you can very soon tell which your future is going to be. The girl who begins making money young will go on making it as a woman. You may find it difficult to do at first, but it will come easier later on; especially if you get your money by hard work.

If you only try to make it by easy means, you are bound to lose after a time. Nobody who makes bets ever wins in the end; it is the bookmaker, the man who receives the bets, that scores over it. Yet there are thousands of fools who go on putting their money on, because they won a bit once or hope to win some day.

Any number of poor girls have become rich, but in nearly every case it was because they meant to do so from the first; they worked for it, and put every penny they could make into the bank to begin with, and saved up. So each one of you has the chance, if you like to take it. The great owner of millions, John Jacob Astor, began his career as a poor boy-pedlar with seven German flutes as his stock-in-trade. He sold them for more than he gave, and went on increasing his business.

By saving up, you have the more to give in charity, and it enables you to keep yourself and not to be a burden to others. It is also good as an example to others. Begin saving at once.

MOTTO.—"Don't put all your eggs into one basket," so don't give all your work to one trade.

Start a money-box, put any money you can make into that, and when you have got a fair amount in it, hand it over to a bank, and start an account for yourself. As a first-class Scout, you have to have a certain amount in the savings bank before you can become entitled to wear a badge. Two cents a week is more than a dollar a year.

Employment

STICK TO IT, the thrush sings. One of our worst diseases nowadays is that people don't seem to have the energy to stick to what they have to do; they try a change. This is a fatal mistake. Whatever you take up, do it with all your might, and *stick to it*.

You may say you can't manage two professions at a time, or as Sir Boyle Roche said, "I am not like a bird, able to be in two places at once" (this is really an enviable state, and I hope the bird appreciates the privilege). Still, when you have work to do, there are often spare spaces which might be filled in with some other paying occupation.

Supposing you had a fancy to have a lot of money (and it is not a thing to be sneezed at), or if you ever had to earn your own livelihood, there are many ways you could get it, provided that your head is screwed on the right way. Besides nursing, teaching, typewriting, post-office, or clerk, there are many less crowded

AGNES BADEN POWELL.

employments such as hairdressing, making flowers, coloring photographs or retouching, teaching gymnastics, dentist's assistant, librarian, bookkeeping, or shorthand reporting, besides crafts like carving, bookbinding, or lace-making. Women gardeners are now earning good wages. There are colleges in which they are trained and they work in hothouses with great success.

But before any new employment can be taken up, you must begin by learning about it now, so "pave the way." Lay out your plans, and begin collecting information. You will not have any luck unless you try hard. "Heaven only helps those who help themselves." "Luck is like a street-car: the only way to get it is to look out for every chance and seize it—run at it and jump on—don't sit down and wait for it to pass. Opportunity is a street-car which has very few stopping-places."

CHOOSE A CAREER.—"Be prepared" for what is going to happen to you in the future. If you are in a situation where you are earning money, think what you are going to do when you finish that job. You ought to be learning some proper trade to take up; and save your pay in the meantime, to keep you going till you get employment in your new trade.

And try to learn something of a second trade, in case the first one fails you at any time, as so very often happens.

An employer told me once that he never engaged a lad who carried his mouth open (boys who breathe through the mouth are generally stupid).

"Keep your mouth shut" is a good motto, not only so as not to breathe in dust and the seeds of disease, but also so as not to say things hastily that you will have to repent later on.

Being punctual is also a most important thing if you want to keep your place. Employment is given to the punctual ones. Rushing is not punctuality. Punctuality means—having everything ready beforehand. It does not mean running *after* the bell rings, but being ready waiting for the bell.

Careers

Really well-educated women can make a good income by taking up translating, dispensing to a doctor or in a hospital, as stockbrokers, house decorators, or agents, managers of laundries, accountants, architects. In the new libraries at Deptford girls will now take the place of boys as assistants.

In an examination in architecture three women gained diplomas, the head of these was classed first with two men, out of twenty-three candidates.

In Russia the municipal fire brigade has been commanded by a young lady, Mlle. Yermoloff. She obtained the special permission of the Czar to join this splendidly equipped brigade seven years ago, and has risen to fill the head place.

The medical profession is one which needs very hard study for many years, and even then long years of waiting before success comes.

Nursing is more easy, and is of the greatest advantage at the same time, for "every woman is a better wife and a better mother for having been a nurse first."

Even so long ago as the first century women devoted their lives to doctoring, like Zenais, a relation of St. Paul, Leonilla, and Hildegarde of Mont Rupert. Later, Nicerate, in 404, studied medicine and practised with great ability. There is a grand career open to girls now which formerly was impossible for them. Fifty years ago no woman could be made a doctor, though now it is within the power of any girl with perseverance and close study to enter the medical profession, and even to rise up to distinction as a doctor and to honorable celebrity.

What must have been the difficulties and insuperable

HELP THEIR COUNTRY

obstacles for the first few ladies who embarked on a medical career!

In the United States Miss Mabel Boardman has taken charge of the Red Cross work with conspicuous success, and the whole world has benefited by her talent for organizing and carrying out the work.

Throughout Europe Miss Agnes Baden-Powell is known by her Girls' Movement which has brought happiness to thousands of girls.

In speaking of Woman's Work for Fifty Years, Miss Grace Dodge has devoted her time to perfecting the development of the Young Women's Christian Association and her work entitles her to be placed among those who have successfully helped women.

MRS. GARRETT ANDERSON

Mrs. Garrett Anderson is also a very clever lady doctor, possessed of untiring energy. When studying for the medical profession, which no woman had then attempted to do, she had to go to France and work entirely in French to get a doctor's degree. Her great success and her zeal in starting the Hospital for Women, in which all the doctors are women, has been a benefit to hundreds of women. Owing to the confidence felt in her high-principled character, she has been honored by being chosen Mayoress of Aldeburgh. Mrs. Garrett Anderson's example is a great encouragement to all girls, holding out hopes of a great career for them.

ILLUSTRIOUS WOMEN

I mentioned just now that Mme. Curie had done such wonderful work in chemistry, and the Academy of Paris have long debated whether she should not be made an academician for her discoveries in connection with polonium and radium. Lady Huggins is not less talented as an astronomer, musician, and artist. Her great work has been finding out about the smallest stars, what they are made of, whether they are coming towards us or are moving away, and she is a most expert photographer of the stars.

Flying Women

The numbers of women who have taken up aviation prove that women's nerves are good enough for flying.

Madame Dutrieu has made some splendid flights across country over hills and rivers, and lately she took a passenger with her in her biplane. What must be so delightful are the long oversea flights she makes. Baroness de la Roche is a brave flyer, and was the first woman to qualify as a pilot. Amongst other aviatresses are Miss Valentine Ducis, Miss Steir, Miss Marvinzt, Mme. Pettier, Mrs. Newlett, who has many pupils, and Miss Kavanagh, who wears a red cloth costume and a tight red cap when on her monoplane. Mrs. Harbord and Miss Bacon both go in for ballooning, and many delightful lectures Miss Bacon has given, telling of her experiences.

Aviation is a splendid means of tracking and observation, but for driving you require a great deal of endurance, besides a cool head and clear judgment. Then a knowledge of steering by a map or stars is needed. They say it is advisable to have a try-plane before you get a buy-plane.

When you are waiting for a calm day for your aviation, should a hurricane continue to blow, you will generally find that when the gale goes down a great calm comes for twenty-four hours; but do not depend on it, for after that the gale generally comes up again, and then blows harder than ever. You have to know a great deal about the air currents and weather wisdom.

In the course of your reading you will notice that

HELP THEIR COUNTRY

many of the greatest movements for the good of people, and those which have influenced the world most, have been the work of *one* person.

One individual often does more than a whole government or an army. One of you girls may some day alter the lives of hundreds of thousands of people. You know how one man invented printing; one woman started nursing the wounded as a profession for women; one man discovered America; one man invented steam-engines; Galileo invented the telescope; Luther changed the life of Europe. So when you get an idea that will do good, follow it up, and don't fear that because it is only you that it cannot succeed.

Welcome all obstacles, as it is only by meeting with difficulties that you can know how to overcome them and Be Prepared for others in the future.

Hints to Instructors

This camp yarn opens to instructors a wide field for the most important work of all in this scheme of Girl Scouts, and gives them an opportunity for doing really valuable work for the nation. The prevailing want of religion should be remedied by a practical working religion rather than a too spiritual one at first.

SUNDAY.—*In Christian countries all Girl Scouts should without fail, attend Church or Chapel, or a Church Parade or Prayers of their own, on Sunday mornings. The afternoon should then be devoted to the study of God in Nature, by exploring for plants or insects, stalking or observing animals or birds; or in town or bad weather visiting good picture galleries, museums, concerts, etc.; also angel missions, such as visiting sick people, or minding babies, doing good turns by collecting flowers and taking them to patients in hospitals, reading newspapers to the patients, and so on. Sunday is a day of rest; exercise is rest. Change of occupation, from the workshop to the fields, is rest; but the Sabbath is too often a day of loafing, and, morally, the worst day in the whole week for our lads and girls. Arrange discussions on principles (described farther on), and practise good turns on God's day.*

SELF-IMPROVEMENT.—*The instructor's chance now is to encourage the young to look out for themselves. A great deal of poverty comes from trusting to luck and loafing with no knowledge of any other line but their own.*

Part VI

ORGANIZATION

Local Organization

LOCAL ORGANIZATION consists of a Lady Commissioner of the District, Lady Vice-President, Chairman and Vice-Chairman, Secretary and Honorary Treasurer.

The duty of the Lady Commissioner is to encourage the patrols in her neighborhood and further the movement.

Committees

The duty of the Girl Scouts' committee will be:

a. To nominate suitable persons to act as captains, and recommend them to headquarters for official warrants.

b. To register all captains, companies, and patrols in the district at headquarters, at . . . . on payment of 25 cents.

c. To generally supervise and encourage the movement in the district with the least possible amount of interference with the independence and initiative of the companies and patrols.

d. To be responsible for the granting of all Scout badges and awards in its district. Applications for these to be made to the secretary, to whom alone they will be issued by headquarters.

e. The local committee has the power to suspend any captain or lieutenant, or to withhold recognition from any company, patrol, or Scout within its area for grave dereliction of duty, or for disloyalty to the rules of the

Scout movement. Any case of suspension must be at once reported to the secretary at headquarters.

f. Periodical meetings should be held. A suitable quorum should be arranged, according to local conditions.

g. If local by-laws are adopted, two copies must be sent to headquarters—the one for filing, the other for approval and return.

h. To apply for and award captains' signed warrants. Captains and officers may be invited to meet committees from time to time to give details.

Power of Captains

A Captain of a company, has the power to enroll Scouts and to recommend them to the local committee for badges and medals. She also has the power to release a Scout from her promise, and to withdraw her badges at any time, and to discharge her. A Scout who considers herself unjustly treated may appeal to the local committee; their decision will be final.

A Scout discharged for misconduct, or one who deserts from her company or patrol, is no longer entitled to wear the uniform or badges of the Girl Scouts, and must return them. She cannot attend parades and displays. Captains should not accept as recruits girls from other organizations, clubs, or schools, unless by the desire of their own officer.

A girl must not join a different patrol without the written consent of her captain.

A captain appoints her own lieutenants and patrol leaders for one year, when she can either reappoint them or substitute others. She can at any time reduce a patrol leader to corporal or to Scout. Captains have a free hand in all interior administration.

Where no committee exists, patrols of Girl Scouts should write to the headquarters' office to be enrolled, and if badges are required, letters from three well-known

HELP THEIR COUNTRY

people should be sent up, and any further information or advice will readily be given. Enrollment cards are supplied and pamphlets can be had on application, also forms for nomination of officers, at Headquarters,

A Company consists of three or more patrols.

A Captain is an officer who has charge of a company, and must be over the age of twenty-one.

A Lieutenant is an assistant to the Captain.

A Patrol Leader is a Scout appointed by a Captain (or by vote of the patrol where no Captain exists) to command a patrol for one year and should be over fifteen.

A Corporal is a Scout selected by the patrol leader to be her assistant, and to take command of the patrol when she herself is away.

A Chaplain is a pastor appointed to superintend the religious training of a company.

A Scout should be between the ages of ten and sixteen, and is either First Class, Second Class, or Tenderfoot.

A Second Class Scout is one who has passed certain tests (see page 123), and can then go in for proficiency badges.

A Tenderfoot is a girl who has joined the Girl Scouts, but has not yet passed her tests for second class Scout.

In special cases girls may become Junior Tenderfoots at a younger age, in separate patrols.

No Scout can be enrolled without showing the written consent of parent or guardian.

A Court of Honor is formed of the Captain and two patrol leaders or in the case of a single patrol by the patrol leader and the corporal. It decides rewards, penalties, and other questions.

Scouts are sent out to track or other work in pairs, and never go scouting or marching with boys, and are forbidden while on duty to speak without leave to boys.

Scouts should not do or wear anything to be conspicuous, and need not carry staves unless on parade, or for ambulance practice.

Captains and lieutenants obtain an official signed warrant from headquarters.

Scouts obtain an official enrollment card.

Companies obtain an ornamental registration card.

The Girl Scouts' Corps belong to no party, no politics, and is non-denominational.

Uniform

Uniform for Girl Scouts is not compulsory. Scouts should, as far as possible, dress alike, especially in each patrol, as regards hat, necktie, and color of blouse.

Hat. Dark blue scout's felt, flat wide brim, with chin-strap or elastic. A band with monogram can be had.

Neckerchief. Pale blue, forty inches, worn knotted at the throat, and also at the ends, till the good turn is done. (It makes a good sling for First Aid, stretcher, or rope, bandage, or signal flag.)

Shirt Blouse. Of company color, with patrol crest sewn on left front. Two pockets.

Skirt. Dark blue serge, two flap pockets. Dark blue knickers.

Stockings. Dark blue woolen, or black, worn drawn up tight over the knee.

Badge. Enameled monogram brooch, or necktie. Officers' dress should be plain, nothing conspicuous.

Lieutenant

The uniform is the same as the captain's, with three white stripes in chevrons on the left sleeve. The badge is the brass monogram, and is worn on the necktie.

Patrol leader carries a staff with the flag, having the patrol flower emblem on it. Two white chevrons on left sleeve below the badge.

Corporal has one white stripe on left sleeve.

Captains, lieutenants, patrol leaders, and corporals

HELP THEIR COUNTRY 123

wear "bos'ns" whistles for signaling and calling, as well as to join the band when marching.

Girl Scouts only wear their uniform when the patrol meets.

QUALIFICATION FOR THE THREE GRADES OF GIRL SCOUTS

The Tests

A Tenderfoot (Badge, a Brooch), must be ten years old (in few cases, girls are admitted younger).

Before making the Scout Promise, she must know:

How to tie four of the following knots: reef, sheet-bend, clove hitch, bowline, fisherman's and sheep-shank (see p. 30–32).

Must know Governor of their State and Mayor of their city.

The History of the Flag, and how to fly it (see p. 102).

A Second Class Girl Scout (Badge, worn on left arm), must have joined and had one month's service as Third Class Scout. She must pass the following tests:

Must have made a drawing or cut out and made in cloth or on paper the Flag of the United States (see p. 102).

Know how to cook one simple dish, such as a potato or a quarter of a pound of meat.

Lay a fire in stove, or light a fire in the open with two matches.

Make a bed properly, and know how to make an invalid's bed.

Know her own measurements (see cards at Headquarters, for detail of measurement) (see p. 74).

Must know the eight points of the compass (see compass, page 58).

Must know what to do in case of fire (see p. 91).

Must know remedy for poison ivy or what to do to prevent frost-bite (see p. 101).

Must know how to work a buttonhole, or knit, or crochet.

A First Class Girl Scout. Badge (sewn on left sleeve above elbow which entitles the wearer to go in for all round cords).

Must have gained a Second Class Badge.

Must know how to lay a table properly for breakfast, dinner, and supper.

Bring a shirtwaist or skirt sewn by herself or equivalent needlework.

Be able to describe how to get to a place and walk two miles in one hour.

Must be able to dress and wash a child of two years old or younger (see page 88).

Must have an elementary knowledge of first aid to the injured, viz.: how to save life in two of the following accidents (allotted by two examiners): Fire, page 91; or revive apparently drowned persons, page 95; runaway horses, page 96; sewer gas, page 97; or bandage an injured patient, pages 97–98.

Must have elementary knowledge of signaling and of semaphore code, or Morse alphabet (page 37).

Must have fifty cents in savings bank, earned by herself.

Must bring a girl trained by herself in tests, Tenderfoot Class Girl Scout.

Know how to distinguish and name three trees, three flowers, three animals, three birds.

Must know simple laws of sanitation, page 66; health, pages 70 to 73, and ventilation, must pass First Aid Examination as per Red Cross First Aid Handbook.

Swim fifty yards in her clothes or show a list of twelve satisfactory good turns.

Show points of compass without a compass, must give correctly the Scouts' secret pass words.

HELP THEIR COUNTRY

The subjects for proficiency badges can be taken up after a girl becomes a Second Class Girl Scout, and the interest in her work is thus continued. The badges for proficiency are registered and can be issued only at Headquarters.

ENROLLMENT

Ceremony of Investiture of Scouts

Ceremonial for a Tenderfoot to be invested as a Scout should be a serious and earnest function. The Captain calls "Fall in." The patrol is formed in a horseshoe, with Captain and lieutenant in the gap, and the American flag spread out. The Tenderfoot, with her patrol leader (who will already have taught her tests and knots), stands just inside the circle, opposite the captain. "Salute." All salute her. The lieutenant holds the staff and hat, shoulder knot and badge, and neckerchief of the Tenderfoot. When ordered to come forward by the captain, the patrol leader then brings the Tenderfoot to the center. The Captain then asks: "Do you know what your honor means?"

The Tenderfoot replies: "Yes, it means that I can be trusted to be truthful and honest." (Or words to that effect). Captain: "Can I trust you on your honor—

1. "To be loyal to God and the country?
2. "To try and do daily good turns to other people?"

The Tenderfoot then makes the half salute, and so do the whole company, whilst she says: "I promise, on my honor—

1. "To be loyal to God and the country.
2. "To try and do daily good turns to other people."

The Captain then says: "I trust you, on your honor, to keep this promise."

Whilst the recruit is making her promises aloud, all the

Scouts remember their own promises, and vow anew to keep them.

The Captain orders: "Invest."

The patrol leader then steps out, gives her staff, and puts on her hat, neckerchief, and knot.

She then marches up the line to the captain, who pins on her trefoil badge, and explains that it is her Scout's "life." If, for misbehavior, her trefoil or life has to be taken from her, she becomes a dead Scout for the time the captain orders—a day or a week—and is in disgrace. The badge can be worn at all times, but the uniform is worn only when the patrol meets. The recruit then faces about, and salutes the patrol.

Retiring to the end of the line, the Scout is given the full salute and present staves.

The new Scout is then initiated into the mysteries of the Girl Scouts' secret signs, the handshake, and the secret passwords *Be Prepared, said backwards*. The captain orders: "To your patrol—quick march."

The patrol shoulder staves; the new Scout and her patrol leader march back to their places.

These badges being the registered designs of the Corps, do not *belong* to the girls who have passed the tests.

The equipment does not belong to the girl unless by special permission.

Any person wearing Girl Scouts' badges without permission is liable to be prosecuted according to law, and may incur a penalty. Offenses, such as people who are not enrolled saluting, outsiders wearing Girl Scouts' badges, or "Monkey" patrols wearing Girl Scouts' uniforms, must be dealt with by trial at a Court of Honor to determine the forfeit or penalties to be imposed on the culprits.

Captains have the power to dismiss a Scout, and the badge and uniform must then be returned. If the girl has paid for her uniform the money must be refunded on return of her uniform.

HELP THEIR COUNTRY

When to Wear the Badge

A little girl asked me what were the occasions when she might wear her badge, thinking it was not for everyday use. But I told her, "You can wear your badge any day and any hour when you are doing what you think is right. It is only when you are doing wrong that you must take it off; as you would not then be keeping your Scout promises. Thus you should either take off the badge, or stop doing what you think is wrong."

The tests for badges given here are liable to be altered when it is expedient. It will be noticed that some of the tests for Girl Scouts are more difficult than the same subjects for Boy Scouts. On the other hand, some of those for Boy Scouts are not adapted for Girl Scouts.

The " Thanks " Badge

As already described, you can give the "Thanks" badge to any one to whom you owe gratitude.

Medals for Meritorious Deeds

To obtain one of these will be the ambition of every Girl Scout.

These medals are only granted by headquarters, or by the president in a colony, on special recommendation from the captain, who should send in a full account with written evidence from two witnesses of the case, through the local committee, if one exists.

These are worn on the right breast, and are awarded as follows:

Life-Saving Medals

Bronze Cross (Red Ribbon). Presented as the highest possible award for gallantry. It can only be won where the claimant has shown special heroism or has faced extraordinary risk of life in saving life.

Silver Cross (Blue Ribbon). For gallantry, with considerable risk to herself.

Badge of Merit (Gilt Wreath. White Ribbon). For a Scout who does her duty exceptionally well, though without grave risks to herself, or for twenty marks awarded by her captain for various specially good actions, or for specially good work in recruiting on behalf of the Girl Scout movement. Full records of such deeds must be kept by the captain to accompany the claim.

How to Become a " Silver Fish "

A Girl Scout must win the following badges: Ambulance (and First Aid), Clerk, Cook, Child-Nurse, Dairymaid, Florist, Fire Brigade, Gymnast, Interpreter, Laundress, Matron, Musician, Needlewoman, Naturalist, Sick Nurse, Pathfinder, Pioneer, Signaler, Swimmer.

In examining for tests one of the committee should, if possible, be present.

The Local Committee should be satisfied, through the recommendation of the girls' Captain, that the tests were satisfactorily performed.

N. B. The rule is that the examiners may not lay claim to any articles produced as tests, such as tarts, cakes, flags, knickers, etc.

It is contemplated to award special higher badges to Girl Scouts who pass their tests through classes at Continuation or Evening Classes.

TESTS FOR PROFICIENCY BADGES

The Captain of each Patrol recommends the girl who deserves a Proficiency Badge. Girls who have attained Second Class Rank can obtain these Badges for proficiency after passing the necessary tests before two qualified and independent examiners or before a Court of Honor.

In districts where no committee exists, a Captain can obtain Proficiency Badges for girls who deserve them by applying direct to Headquarters. In such cases the Captain's recommendation is sufficient.

LIST OF BADGES TO BE GAINED

(Proficiency Badges)

Attendance, Annual. (Badge, Palm Leaf) awarded when a scout has completed a year's attendance.

Ambulance (White Cross):

To obtain a badge for Ambulance a Girl Scout must have a knowledge of the Schaefer methods of resuscitation in cases of drowning (see page 95).

What to do in case of fire (see page 91).

How to stop a runaway horse (see page 96).

Treatment and Bandaging the Injured (see page 97).

How to stop bleeding (see page 100).

How to apply a tourniquet (see page 100).

Treatment of Ivy Poison (see page 100).

Treatment of frost-bite (see page 101).

How to remove cinder from eye (see page 90).

Artist (Palette).

To obtain an Artist's badge a girl must draw or paint in oils or water colors from nature; or model in clay or plasticine or modeling wax from cartoons or from life.

Or,

Arts and Crafts: Carve in wood, work in metals, cabinet work.

† **Boatswain** (Life Buoy).:

To obtain seamanship badge a Girl Scout must be able to tie six knots (see page 30).

To be able to row, pole, scull, or steer a boat.

Child-Nurse (Green Cross):

To obtain this Badge a Girl Scout must take care of a child for two hours each day for a month, or care for a baby for one hour a day for a month.

Examination should be made with infant present, if possible.

Must have had charge of child by herself; should understand care of children, elementary instruction (pages 70–72), know three kindergarten games, and describe treatment of simple ailments. Be able to make poultices, and do patching and darning. Know how to test bath heat and use of thermometer, test the pulse (see p. 141).

Clerk (Pen and Paper):

Must have legible handwriting; ability to typewrite; a knowledge of spelling and punctuation; a library hand; or alternately write in shorthand from dictation at twenty words a minute a minimum. Ability to write a letter from memory on the subject given verbally five minutes previously. Knowledge of simple bookkeeping and arithmetic.

HELP THEIR COUNTRY

Cook (Gridiron):
Must know how to wash up, wait on table, light a fire, lay a table for four, and hand dishes correctly at table. Clean and dress a fowl; clean a fish. How to make a cook-place in the open; make tea, coffee, or cocoa, mix dough and bake bread in oven, and state approximate cost of each dish.

Know how to cook two kinds of meat (page 81).

Boil or roast two kinds of vegetables, potatoes, rice and another vegetable (page 83).

How to make two salads.

How to make a preserve of berries or fruit, or to can them.

Invalid Cooking

How to make gruel, barley water, milk toast, oyster or clam soup, beef tea or chicken jelly, kumyss (page 85).

Cyclist (A wheel):
Must own her bicycle; be able to mend a tire; must pledge herself to give the service of her bicycle to the government in case of need.

If she ceases to own a bicyle she must return the badge.

To read a map properly (see page 137).

To know how to repair a tire.

Dairy Maid (Sickle):
Know how to test cow's milk with Babcock Test (page 142).

To make butter.

How to milk.

Know how to do general dairy work (page 84), such as cleaning pans, etc., sterilizing utensils (page 143); know how to feed, kill, and dress poultry.

Cows should be individually selected and Tuberculin tested.

A Scout should have a short course in the analysis of milk. There are many small manuals in use at present and easily available.

See Notes to Instructors (page 142).

† **Electrician** (Badge, Lightning):

Simple battery, fusing, connection of bells and telephones. Understand rescue and resuscitation. Non-conducting substances and insulation.

Farmer:

Incubating chickens, feeding and rearing chickens under hens.

Storing eggs.

Knowledge of bees. Swarming, hiving and use of artificial combs.

Care of pigs. How to cure hams.

See Notes to Instructors (page 142).

† **Flyer** (Badge, Aeroplane):

Pass tests in knowledge of air currents, weather lore. Must have made an aeroplane to fly 25 yards (or have a certificate for driving an aeroplane), and some knowledge of engines.

Health. (Badge, Dumbbell): (Annual.)

Do not chew gum.

Eat no sweets, candy, or cake between meals for three months.

Drink nothing but water for a year (except tea, coffee, chocolate, or cocoa).

Walk a mile daily for three months.

Sleep with open window.

Take a bath or rub all over with a wet towel daily for three months.

HELP THEIR COUNTRY

† **Horsemanship** (Spur):

Demonstrate riding at a walk, trot and gallop.
Know how to saddle and bridle a horse correctly, and how to groom a horse properly.
Know how to harness correctly in a single or double harness, and how to drive.
Know how to tether and hobble, and when to give feed and drink.
State lighting up time.

Hospital Nurse (White Cross):

Must have passed examination for First Aid of Red Cross.
Know how to make an invalid's bed.
Know how to take temperature and how to count the pulse (page 141).

Interpreter (Clasped Hands):

Be able to carry on a simple conversation in any other language beside her own.
Write a letter in a foreign language.
Read or translate a passage from a book or newspaper in French, German, Italian or any other language not her own.

Laundress (Flat Iron):

Know how to wash and iron a garment, clear starch, and how to do up a blouse.
Press a skirt and coat.
Know how to use soap and starch, how to soften hard water, and how to use a wringer.

Matron Housekeeper (Two Keys):

Know how to use a vacuum cleaner. How to stain and polish hardwood floors (see page 142). How to clean wire window screens (see page 142). How to put away fur and flannels (142). How to clean glass, kitchen utensils (page 77), brass and silverware.

Marketing.

Know three different cuts of meat, and prices of each.

Know season for chief fruits and vegetables, fish and game.

Know how flour, sugar, rice, cereals and vegetables are sold; whether by package, pound or bulk, quarts, page 143.

Musical (Harp):

Know how to play a musical instrument. Be able to do sight reading, have a knowledge of note signs and terms.

Name not less than four classical compositions, and to be able to name the composer of each.

Or,

Have a knowledge of singing, have a pleasing voice, and must have had some voice training.

Name not less than four Grand Operas, and name the composer of each.

Naturalist (Flower):

Make a collection of sixty species of wild flowers, ferns and grasses, and correctly name them.

Or,

Colored drawings of wild flowers, ferns or grasses drawn by herself.

Twelve sketches or photographs of animal life (birds and animals).

HELP THEIR COUNTRY

Name and describe sixty wild birds, or be able to describe sixty animals, insects, or reptiles, either in woods or in zoölogical garden, and give particulars of their lives, habits, appearance, etc. Markings of twenty of them.

Needlewoman (Scissors):

Know how to cut and fit. How to sew by hand and by machine.

Know how to knit, embroider, or crochet.

Bring two garments made and cut out by herself; and sew on hooks and eyes and buttons. Make a button hole, and bring examples of darning and patching.

Pathfinder (Hand):

Know the topography of the city, all the public buildings, public schools, and monuments. Know how to call up the fire alarm.

To be able to state the direction by Stars or the Sun (page 58).

† **Pioneer** (Axes):

Tie six knots. Make a camp kitchen. Build a shack of one kind or another suitable for three occupants.

† **Rifle-shot** (Badge, Rifles):

Pass tests in judging distances, 300 and 600 yards. Miniature rifle shooting, any position. 20 rounds at 15 or 25 yards. 80 out of 100.

Signaling (Two Flags):

Send and receive a message in two of the following systems of signaling: Semaphore, Morse. Not fewer than twenty-four letters a minute.

Swimmer (Life Buoy):

Swim fifty yards in clothes, skirt and boots. Demonstrate diving, artificial respiration (page 95), flinging a life-line, flinging a life-buoy, saving the drowning (page 92).

Requirements or examination must be sent to parents of candidate for permission. Must also be obtained from the family physician or some other doctor.

† **Telegraphist** (Badge, Telegraph Post).

Elementary electricity; able to read and send Morse code.

EXTRA.—A First Class Girl Scout can obtain the following extra badges:—The "Attendance" badge, for each year's attendance. The "Nursing Sister" Red Cross armlet, for passing Hospital Nurse, Cook, Matron, Laundress, having already obtained. Ambulance— The "All-Round-Shoulder Cords" can be worn by a "First Class Girl Scout for passing any seven of the above tests, and show a flag made by herself. The Order of the "Silver Fish" is presented for passing all, except those marked ✕, which are extra. The honorary "Silver Fish" is presented for exceptional services.

HELP THEIR COUNTRY 137

How to Read a Map

Conventional Signs & Lettering Used in Field Sketching

Conventional Signs enable you to give information on

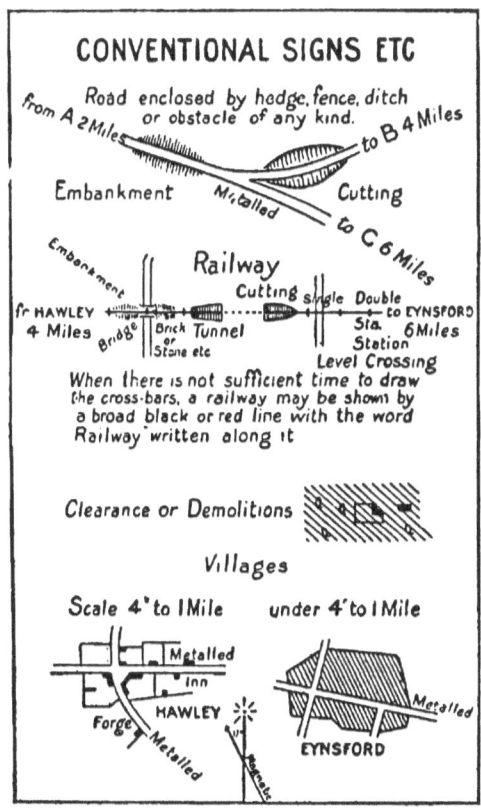

a sketch or map in a simple manner which is easily understood. In addition to the sign it is often necessary to give an additional description, *e. g.*, whether a railway is double or single, the width of roads, the nature of woods (Oak, Pine, etc.), etc., as shown on the following pages.

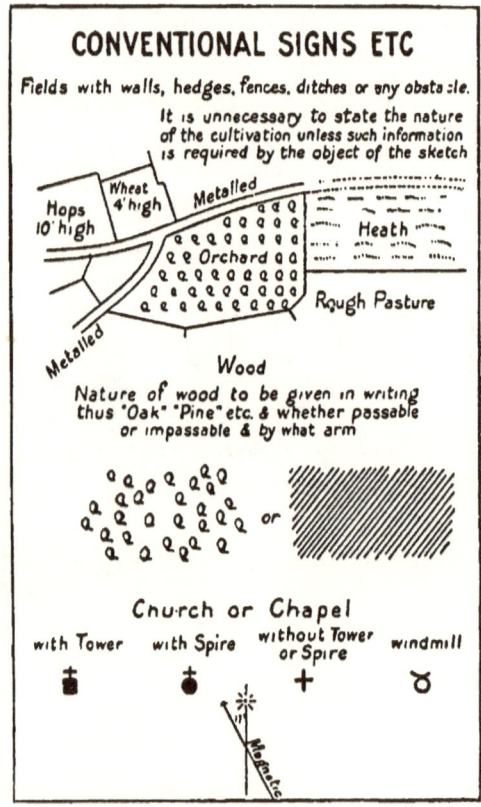

Whatever lettering is used should be legible and not interfere with the detail of the sketch. All lettering should be horizontal, except the names of roads, railways, rivers and canals, which should be written along them.

HELP THEIR COUNTRY 139

Remember to fill in the North point on your sketch, as it is useless without it. Leave a margin of about an inch all round your sketch and state the scale that you have made your sketch, *e. g.*, two inches to the mile.

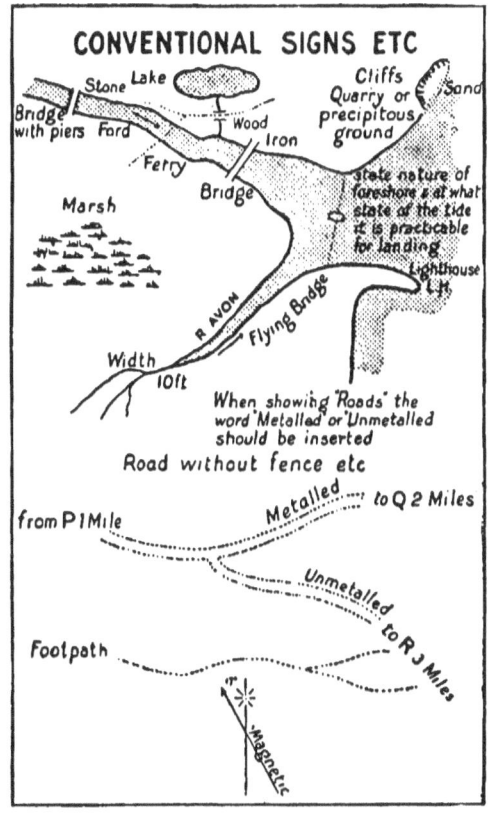

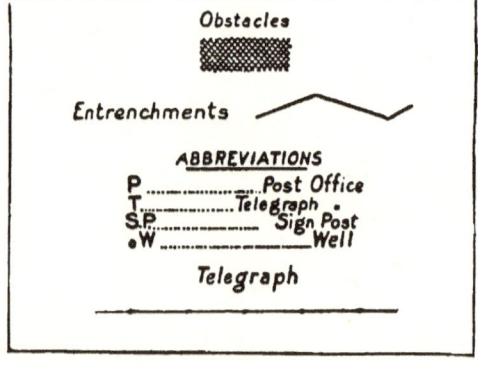

HELP THEIR COUNTRY

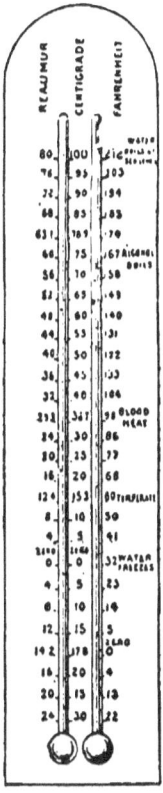

Thermometers

To convert a given number of degrees Fahrenheit into Centigrade, deduct 32, multiply by 5, and divide by 9. To convert into Réaumur, deduct 32, multiply by 4, and divide by 9. To convert degrees Centigrade into Fahrenheit, multiply by 9, divide by 5, and add 32. To convert Réaumur into Fahrenheit, multiply by 9, divide by 4, and add 32.

The diagram shows corresponding degrees.

Beat of Pulse per minute

Pulse beat for normal person:

Infant before age of one year, 130 to 115 beats per minute.

Infant up to two years of age, 115 to 130 beats per minute.

Adult, 70 to 80 beats per minute. Adult in old age, 70 to 60 in normal health.

NOTES TO INSTRUCTORS

How to Clean Wire Window Screens

Rub down with Kerosene oil outside and inside.

Three Primary Colors *are, Red, Blue and Yellow.*

Polishing Floors

One quart of turpentine to one quarter (¼) pound of beeswax. Warm, taking care not to let any fire reach the turpentine. Rub in the floor with flannel and polish with hard brush. A little powdered burnt umber mixed in gives a nice brown stain.

To Put Away Flannels

First thoroughly air and beat them, then wrap up with cedar chips, refuse tobacco, or camphor, and wrap in newspapers, being careful to close every outlet to keep out moths.

Babcock Test

The Babcock test is a test for determining the butter fat in milk.

Bottles are devised which are known as Babcock milk bottles, and are registered to show the per cent. of fat in milk. A certain amount of milk is mixed with a certain amount of Commercial Sulphuric acid of a specific gravity 1.83 which is added by degrees and thoroughly shaken up with the milk. Enough distilled water is added to fill the bottle. The mixture is then centrifuged in a Babcock Centrifuge, and the centrifuged fat read in per cent. on the neck of the bottle.

The Official Travelers' Babcock Test can be purchased from the Creamery Package Manufactory Co., Chicago Ill., and costs between $5.00 and $6.00

All utensils used in dairy work should be sterilized by steaming or boiling for five minutes.

How to Cure Hams

1 tablespoonful of Saltpetre rubbed into the face of each ham; let it remain one day. Literally cover the ham with salt and pack it in a closed box. Leave it in box as many days as there are pounds to the ham.

Take it out, wash in warm water; cover the face of the ham with black pepper, and smoke it ten days with green hickory or red-oak chips.

Farm Weights and Measures

When you want to make a cup of coffee or a small sago pudding, do not be led into buying a "bag" of either.

1 bag of coffee contains about 142 lb.
1 bag of sago contains about 112 lb.
1 bag of sugar contains about 112 lb.
1 bag of walnuts contains about 1 cwt.

1 gallon of honey is 12 lb.
8 lb. of butter is 1 clove.
56 lb. of butter is 1 firkin.
120 lb. of potatoes is 1 cwt.
1 bushel of flour is 56 lb.
1 stone of soda is 14 lb.
1 stone of butcher's meat is 8 lb. only.

Weight of meat on a sheep is about 60 lb.
Weight on meat on a cow is about 450 lb.
Weight of meat on an ox is about 650 lb.

36 trusses of hay in 1 load.
56 lb. of hay (old) in 1 truss.
1 acre of grass will grow about 1½ tons of hay.

> 1 fathom is 6 feet.
> 1 league is 3 miles.
>
> 1 load of tiles is 1000.

INDEX

Accidents, be prepared for, 11
Aeroplanes, 116
America, 103–105
Animals, how to photograph them, 44
——How to study habits, 45
Archery, 42

Babcock test of milk, 142
Badges, 127–129
Bad habits, 106
Bandaging the injured, 97
Bathing, precautions to take against accidents, 28
Birds, study their habits, 47
Boating, 27
Botany, 51
Boxing the compass, 58

Camp, beds, 20
——Cleanliness, 23
——Equipment, 28
——Ground suitable for, 18
——Kitchen, 25
——Orders, 27
——Provisioning, 22
——Routine, 25
——Water, 19
Camp-fire stories, 6–9–10
Camping, 18
Captain, power of, 120
Careers, 114
Care of body, 70
Care of children, 86–88
Chivalry, 3–16
——Of helping others, 106
——Modesty, 108
——Never take tips for voluntary help given, 106

Commands and signals, 38
Commissioner, 119
Committee, 120
Company, 122–123
Compass, 58
Compound fracture, 98–99
Cooking, 80
——Eggs, 80
——Fish, 82
——For invalid, 85
——Meat, 81
——Milk, 84
——Oatmeal, 82
——Vegetables, 83
Corporal, 121
Court of honor, 121
Cows, how to test milk, 142

Deduction or sign, 14–33
Diseases, prevention of, 68
——Microbes, 66
Distances, how to judge, 35
Drowning, rescue, 92

Early rising, 4
Ears, 71
Empress Eugénie's circle, 43
Endurance, 12–75–76
Enrolment, 125
Eyes, 72

Fire, what to do in case of, 91
Fires, forest, 20–91
First aid, 91
——Artificial respiration, 95
——Bleeding in cases of, 90–99
——Broken limbs, 97–98
——Drowning, rescue from, 92
——Fracture, compound, 97–98

145

INDEX

First aid—*Continued*
—Frostbite, 101
—Gas or sewer gas, 97
—Grit in eye, 90
—Ice, rescue, 97
—Ivy poisoning, 101
—Nosebleed, 90
—Runaway horses, 96
Fish, 51
Flag, 102
Flowers, 64
Fortitude, 75

Games, 42
—Charades, 8
—Chasing the owl, 36
—Circus, 43
—Far and near, 36
—Flags, 75
—Inventory, 36
—Kim's, 8
—Morgan's or shop windows, 8
—Scout meets Scout, 8
—Secret despatch, 42
—Stalking the deer, 44–45
—Testing noses, 36
—Turkey and wildcat, 36
Gardening, 63
Girl Scout laws, 3
Good turns, 4, 106
Grades of Scouts, 123

Health, 70–76
Home life, 66
Hospital work, 90
Housewifery, 77
How to secure burglar, 42
How to start a patrol, 1
How to tell time by stars, 56–60

Illustrious women, 115
Insects, 49
Instructors' notes, 26–142

Knots, 30

Laws of Scouts, 3
Lieutenant, 122

Mariner's compass, 59
Measures, farm, 143
Measuring self, 74
Medals, 127
Meetings, 2–7
Memory practice, 36
Milk, 84
Money-making, 111
Morse alphabet, 37

Needlework, 77
North, how to find, 58
Nose-breathing, 71
Notes to instructors, 142

Open-air pursuits, 33
Organization, 119

Path-finding, 62
—By Indian signs, 34
Patriotism, 102
Patrol leader, 121
Physical exercises, 70
Promise of Girl Scouts, 3
Pursuits, 33

Rank of Girl Scouts, 123
Reptiles, 21
Rescue from drowning, 92
Rescue from ice, 97
Runaway horses, 96

Sanitation, 66–68
Saving life, 91
Second-class Girl Scout, 123
Self-defence, 41
Self-dicipline, 106
Self-improvement, 108
Self-measures, 74
Shells, 50
Shooting, 41

INDEX

Sign, 33
Signals—
——Hand signals, 40
——Indian signs, 34
——Scout signs, 41
——Semaphore, 24
——Whistle signals, 39
Snakes, 21
South, how to find, 58
Spooring, 36
Stalking, 33
Stars, 55
Star-spangled banner, 104
Stories, camp-fire, 6–9–10
Sunday, 117
Swimming, 28

Teeth, 72
Tenderfoot, 123
Tests for grade or rank, 123
Tests for proficiency, 129
Thrift, 111
Tidiness, 67
Tourniquet, 100
Tracking, 36
Trees, 52

Uniform, 122

Waste, 110
Water, 69
Woodcraft, 44

www.ingramcontent.com/pod-product-compliance
Lightning Source LLC
Chambersburg PA
CBHW030322080526
44584CB00012B/673